# LDS PERSPECTIVES
## ON THE
# DEAD SEA SCROLLS

# FARMS Publications

Teachings of the Book of Mormon

The Geography of Book of Mormon Events: A Source Book

The Book of Mormon Text Reformatted according to Parallelistic Patterns

Eldin Ricks's Thorough Concordance of the LDS Standard Works

A Guide to Publications on the Book of Mormon: A Selected Annotated Bibliography

Book of Mormon Authorship Revisited: The Evidences for Ancient Origins

Ancient Scrolls from the Dead Sea: Photographs and Commentary on a Unique Collection of Scrolls

LDS Perspectives on the Dead Sea Scrolls

*Periodicals*

Insights: An Ancient Window

FARMS Review of Books

Journal of Book of Mormon Studies

*FARMS Reprint Series*

Book of Mormon Authorship: New Light on Ancient Origins

The Doctrine and Covenants by Themes

## Copublished with Deseret Book Company

An Ancient American Setting for the Book of Mormon

Warfare in the Book of Mormon

By Study and Also by Faith: Essays in Honor of Hugh W. Nibley

The Sermon at the Temple and the Sermon on the Mount

Rediscovering the Book of Mormon

Reexploring the Book of Mormon

Of All Things! Classic Quotations from Hugh Nibley

The Allegory of the Olive Tree

Temples of the Ancient World

Expressions of Faith: Testimonies from LDS Scholars

Feasting on the Word: The Literary Testimony of the Book of Mormon

*The Collected Works of Hugh Nibley*

Old Testament and Related Studies

Enoch the Prophet

The World and the Prophets

Mormonism and Early Christianity

Lehi in the Desert; The World of the Jaredites; There Were Jaredites

An Approach to the Book of Mormon

Since Cumorah

The Prophetic Book of Mormon

Approaching Zion

The Ancient State

Tinkling Cymbals and Sounding Brass

Temple and Cosmos

Brother Brigham Challenges the Saints

## Published through Research Press

Pre-Columbian Contact with the Americas across the Oceans: An Annotated Bibliography

New World Figurine Project, vol. 1

A Comprehensive Annotated Book of Mormon Bibliography

# LDS PERSPECTIVES
## ON THE
# DEAD SEA SCROLLS

### EDITED BY DONALD W. PARRY AND DANA M. PIKE

**The Foundation for Ancient Research
and Mormon Studies
Provo, Utah**

Foundation for Ancient Research and Mormon Studies
P.O. Box 7113
University Station
Provo, Utah 84602

06  05  04  03  02  01  00  99  98  97                    6  5  4  3  2  1

---

**Publisher's Cataloging-in-Publication**
*(Provided by Quality Books, Inc.)*

LDS perspectives on the Dead Sea scrolls / edited by Donald W.
    Parry and Dana M. Pike.—1st ed.
        p. cm.
        Includes bibliographical references and index.
        ISBN: 0-934893-26-8

    1. Dead Sea scrolls—Criticism, interpretation, etc.
2. Church of Jesus Christ of Latter-day Saints—Doctrines.
3. Mormon Church—Doctrines. I. Parry, Donald W. II. Pike,
Dana M. III. Title: Latter-day Saint perspectives on the Dead
Sea scrolls

BM487.L37 1997              296.1'55
                            QBI97-40730

# CONTENTS

# ILLUSTRATIONS

# INTRODUCTION

Latter-day Saints love ancient religious records. We have dozens of them in the Bible under such names as Genesis, Judges, Ruth, Isaiah, and John. Through the Prophet Joseph Smith a great number of other ancient records were restored—the books of Nephi, Alma, Mormon, and Moroni in the Book of Mormon, as well as Abraham and selections from the book of Moses in the Pearl of Great Price. In addition, we anticipate the coming forth of the "words of the lost tribes of Israel" (2 Nephi 29:13) and other ancient texts that have been authored by such individuals as Adam, Enoch, and Joseph.

It is no wonder, then, that since the discovery in 1947 of a large collection of scrolls along the shores of the Dead Sea, many Latter-day Saints have developed a particular interest in what are now known as the Dead Sea Scrolls. The scrolls, of course, do not contain the lost records we await, but they do provide new information about the transmission of the Bible, the Hebrew and Aramaic languages, and the variety of beliefs and practices of the Jews in the late Second Temple period (200 B.C. to A.D. 70).

Interest in the scrolls continues into the 1990s. During the past few years, several LDS scholars have become directly involved in the translation, study, and electronic preservation of the scrolls. In response to LDS interest in the scrolls Brigham Young University's College of Religious Education and the Foundation for Ancient Research and Mormon Studies (FARMS) jointly hosted a conference entitled "LDS Perspectives on the Dead Sea Scrolls," held 23 March 1996 on the BYU campus.

The conference featured seven presentations, versions of which are published in this volume. They discuss the Dead Sea Scrolls and the Messiah, the Book of Mormon, the Bible, the plan of salvation, prayer and worship, and a DNA analysis of the scrolls. With the exception of the keynote address, delivered by world-renowned scrolls scholar Professor Florentino García Martínez, all the presentations were delivered by Latter-day Saints who are BYU or FARMS scholars. An additional article, authored by Andrew Skinner of BYU and written especially for this volume, provides a general introduction to the discovery and contents of the scrolls and related matters.

The various opinions expressed in this volume do not necessarily reflect the views of the editors, Brigham Young University, FARMS, or the Church of Jesus Christ of Latter-day Saints.

## Scroll Terminology

Scroll terminology is not complicated, just abbreviated. The numbers 1–11 designate the cave in which the document was found, the Q stands for Qumran, and the last number indicates the fragment number. For example, 4Q161 was found in Qumran Cave 4 and is fragment number 161. Over the history of scroll scholarship, the same scroll has sometimes been known by various names. This numbering system attempts to clarify the scroll designations, and in this volume we have tried to cross reference each scroll name to avoid confusion.

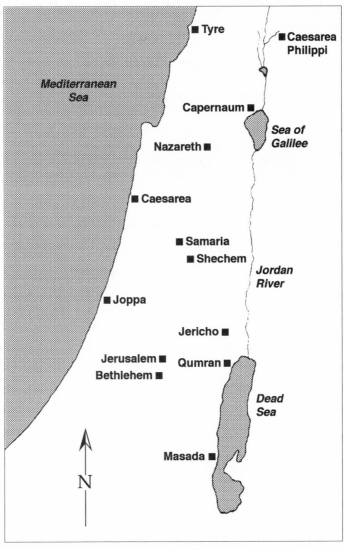

Qumran it its greater geographical context. (Map by Jeff Jolley.)

The Dead Sea Scrolls are very fragmented, and scholars often have to calculate what was written because sections of text both large and small are missing or illegible. In this volume, several different symbols indicate certain types of text restorations. Following is a list of those symbols and their meanings:[1]

| | |
|---|---|
| [xxx] | Text restored by the translator |
| [. . .] | Lacuna of unspecified length in the manuscript |
| /xxx/ | Legible text inserted between the lines by the copyist |
| /. . ./ | Illegible text inserted between the lines by the copyist |
| *Blank* | Space left blank in the manuscript, either unintentionally (new paragraph) or by mistake |
| (xxx) | Editorial insertion by the translator |
| {xxx} | Editorial insertion by the author in this volume |

## Overview of Recent Involvement of Latter-day Saints with Dead Sea Scrolls Scholarship

As information on and photographs or transcriptions of the Dead Sea Scrolls slowly became available in the years following their discovery in 1947, many people interested in the historical and cultural background of the Bible began to actively investigate the contents and to consider the significance of these two thousand-year-old documents. Chief among Latter-day Saints who began to study the scrolls that were available in the 1950s and 1960s was Hugh Nibley (see the following list of publications by Latter-day Saints). Since that time, Latter-day Saints with varying degrees of training have studied, written, and spoken about the value of the scrolls and the interest they have for Latter-day Saints.

Publication of the scrolls slowed considerably in the mid-1960s through mid-1980s. Scholarly and public outcry about the delay in making all of these documents available increased in the late 1980s. In response to this pressure, the Israel Antiquities Authority decided in 1993 to release all the official photographs of scrolls and scroll fragments on microfiche and to take measures to increase the number of scholars working on the official publication of the scrolls in order to hasten the completion of this project. These events have created a renewed interest in the Dead Sea Scrolls around the world. They have also provided an opportunity for several Latter-day Saints associated with BYU and FARMS to participate in research on and in the official publication of some of the Dead Sea Scrolls. The following overview provides highlights of the recent professional activity of Latter-day Saints in research relating to the scrolls.[2]

### 1991

In the fall, Truman G. Madsen, who was then the director of the BYU Jerusalem Center for Near Eastern Studies, was invited to serve as a member of the advisory board of the Dead Sea Scrolls Foundation (DSSF).

### 1992

In the early months of the year, Truman Madsen and William Hamblin, a BYU professor of history teaching at the Jerusalem Center, discussed the possibility that an electronic database of the Dead Sea Scrolls could be created and contacted the Foundation for Ancient Research and Mormon Studies (FARMS), headquartered in Provo, to discuss how that might be accomplished.

Later in the spring, Noel B. Reynolds, president of FARMS and a BYU professor of political science, introduced the possibilities of such a project to Bruce Hafen, then provost of BYU, and a decision was formally made that BYU and FARMS would cooperate on the creation of an electronic database. BYU provided WordCruncher™ computer software necessary for search capabilities, as well as legal and other types of support, and FARMS provided funding, management, electronic versions of the texts, and accepted the responsibility to produce and market the database to the academic community.

In the fall, a preliminary demonstration of Word-Cruncher™ for Windows using a few Dead Sea Scroll texts was shown to Emanuel Tov, editor in chief of *Discoveries in the Judean Desert* (hereafter *DJD*, published by Oxford University Press), the multi-volume series that is the official publication of the Dead Sea Scrolls. Tov was pleased with the possibilities and encouraged the development of the database.

## 1994

In January, while Donald W. Parry, BYU professor of Hebrew and a member of the FARMS board of directors, was living in Jerusalem, Emaunel Tov invited him to become a member of the international team of editors of the Dead Sea Scrolls. Parry is assisting Frank M. Cross, emeritus professor at Harvard University, with work on two Samuel scrolls from Cave 4 at Qumran.

In the spring, David R. Seely, BYU professor of ancient scripture, was invited to become a member of the international team of editors of the Dead Sea Scrolls. Seely is assisting Moshe Weinfeld, a professor at Hebrew University in Jerusalem, with work on the *Barki Nafshi* texts from Cave 4 at Qumran. The results of all their work will be published in *DJD*. Dana M. Pike, BYU professor of ancient scripture, was also invited to become a member of the international team of editors of the Dead Sea Scrolls, and is presently working on miscellaneous and unidentified fragments of scrolls from Cave 4 at Qumran. Steven W. Booras was hired at this time by FARMS as electronic projects manager and specifically assigned to manage the creation of the scroll database.

In the fall, Scott R. Woodward, BYU professor of microbiology, began an academic year at Hebrew University in Jerusalem, with support from the DSSF and FARMS. He helped to establish a lab there to analyze the DNA of scroll fragments and other archaeological artifacts.

(Left to right) BYU Professors Scott R. Woodward, Dana M. Pike, and David Rolph Seely, and Steven W. Booras, FARMS electronic projects manager, in front of the cliffs where Cave 1 is located.

## 1995

Early in the year, Andrew Skinner, BYU professor of ancient scripture, was invited to become a member of the international team of editors of the Dead Sea Scrolls to work with Pike in preparing miscellaneous and unidentified fragments of scrolls from Qumran Cave 4 for publication in *DJD*.

In the spring, BYU and FARMS sponsored a Dead Sea Scrolls conference at the BYU Jerusalem Center for Near Eastern Studies that included the Latter-day Saints that were then actively involved in work on the scrolls. Israeli and other international scroll scholars were invited and a preliminary demonstration of the electronic database was given.

## 1996

During the first few months of the year, FARMS began scanning the negatives of photographs of the Qumran documents held by the Ancient Biblical Manuscripts Center (ABMC), located in Claremont, California. FARMS provided a copy of the digitized images to ABMC in exchange for permission to use the photographs in the database. E. Jan Wilson was at this time hired by FARMS to supervise the electronic formatting of the textual material in the database.

In the spring, BYU's College of Religious Education and FARMS sponsored a one-day conference at BYU that was open to the general public to discuss the scrolls from an LDS point of view. Most of the presentations were by Latter-day Saints actively involved in work on the Dead Sea Scrolls. This volume contains the results of that conference.

In the summer, BYU and FARMS hosted a three day international scholarly conference in Provo on the Dead Sea Scrolls. The program again included presentations by

Latter-day Saints actively involved in Dead Sea Scroll research. Another demonstration of the electronic database, still in the process of development, was given.

Also in the summer, David A. Arnold and David G. Long, BYU professors of electrical engineering, used ground-penetrating radar in the area of the Dead Sea to help archaeologists look for more caves that might contain more scrolls or related material. The results of these tests are not available at press time.

**1997**

In the summer, an international conference will be held in Jerusalem to commemorate the fiftieth anniversary of the discovery of the Dead Sea Scrolls. Latter-day Saint scholars working on the scrolls will be making presentations. It is expected that the electronic database produced by FARMS and BYU will be ready for distribution about this time.

## Select Publications by Latter-day Saints Relating to the Dead Sea Scrolls

The following is a list of publications on the Dead Sea Scrolls by Latter-day Saints during the past four decades. We have listed works by individuals whose scholarship is generally accepted as reputable, although we do not necessarily agree with every point made in all the publications cited. Be aware that since more scrolls have become available for study, it is evident that some of the older publications on the scrolls contain suppositions and pronouncements that are now considered dated or inaccurate. In general, this list does not include comments made about the scrolls in church magazines or the *Church News*, nor publications by Latter-day Saints who have an interest in the scrolls but who are not trained in ancient studies.

**1950s**

Nibley, Hugh W. "More Voices from the Dust." *Instructor* 91 (March 1956): 71–2, 74. Reprinted in *Old Testament and Related Studies*, 239–44. Salt Lake City: Deseret Book and FARMS, 1986.

————. "The Dead Sea Scrolls and the Book of Mormon." In *An Approach to the Book of Mormon*, 135-80. Salt Lake City: Deseret Book, 1957. Reprinted 1964, 1988.

**1960s**

Rogers, Lewis M. "The Dead Sea Scrolls: Qumran Calmly Revisited." *BYU Studies* 2/2 (1960): 109–28.

Nibley, Hugh W. "The Dead Sea Scrolls: Some Questions and Answers." *Instructor* 98 (July 1963): 233–5. Reprinted in *Old Testament and Related Studies*, 245–52. Salt Lake City: Deseret Book and FARMS, 1986.

————. "Qumran and the Companions of the Cave." *Revue de Qumran* 5 (April 1965): 177–98. Reprinted as "Qumran and the Companions of the Cave: The Haunted Wilderness." In *Old Testament and Related Studies*, 253–84. Salt Lake City: Deseret Book and FARMS, 1986.

————. *Since Cumorah*. Salt Lake City: Deseret Book, 1967. Reprinted 1988.

Tvedtnes, John A. "The Dead Sea Scrolls." In *The Church of the Old Testament*, 75–105. Salt Lake City: Deseret Book, 1967. Reprinted 1980.

**1970s**

Nibley, Hugh W. "From the Dead Sea Scrolls." Appendix 1 of *The Message of the Joseph Smith Papyri*, 255–62. Salt Lake City: Deseret Book, 1975.

————. "Churches in the Wilderness." In *Nibley on the Timely and the Timeless*, 155–86. Provo: BYU Religious Studies Center, 1978. Reprinted in *The Prophetic Book of Mormon*, 289–327. Salt Lake City: Deseret Book and FARMS, 1989.

**1980s**

Brown, S. Kent. "The Dead Sea Scrolls: A Mormon Perspective." *BYU Studies* 23/1 (1983): 49–66.

**1990s**

Cloward, Robert A. "Dead Sea Scrolls: LDS Perspective." In *The Encyclopedia of Mormonism*, edited by Daniel H. Ludlow et al., 1:363–364. New York: Macmillan, 1992.

Nibley, Hugh W. "Apocryphal Writings and Teachings of the Dead Sea Scrolls." In *Temple and Cosmos*, 264–335. Salt Lake City: Deseret Book and FARMS, 1992. (Previously unpublished presentation given in 1967 at a seminary graduation.)

Ricks, Stephen D. "Who Wrote the Dead Sea Scrolls?" FARMS, 1993.

García Martínez, Florentino, and Donald W. Parry, eds. *A Bibliography of the Finds in the Desert of Judah 1970–95.* Leiden: E. J. Brill, 1996.

Parry, Donald W. "4QSam[a] and the Tetragrammaton." In *Current Research & Technological Developments on the Dead Sea Scrolls*, edited by Donald W. Parry and Stephen D. Ricks, 106–25. Leiden: E. J. Brill, 1996.

Parry, Donald W. "Retelling Samuel: Echoes of the Books of Samuel in the Dead Sea Scrolls." *Revue de Qumran* 17 (1996): 293–306.

Parry, Donald W., and Steven W. Booras. "The Dead Sea Scrolls CD-ROM Database Project." In *Current Research & Technological Developments on the Dead Sea Scrolls*, edited by Donald W. Parry and Stephen D. Ricks, 239–50. Leiden: E. J. Brill, 1996.

Pike, Dana M. "The Book of Numbers at Qumran: Texts and Context." In *Current Research & Technological Developments on the Dead Sea Scrolls*, edited by Donald W. Parry and Stephen D. Ricks, 166–93. Leiden: E. J. Brill, 1996.

Pike, Dana M. "The 'Congregation of YHWH' in the Bible and at Qumran." *Revue de Qumran* 17 (1996): 233–40.

Seely, David R. "The *Barki Nafshi* Texts *(4Q434–439)*." In *Current Research & Technological Developments on the Dead Sea Scrolls*, edited by Donald W. Parry and Stephen D. Ricks, 194-214. Leiden: E. J. Brill, 1996.

Seely, David R. "The 'Circumcised Heart' in *4Q434 Barki Nafshi*." *Revue de Qumran* 17 (1996): 527–35.

Woodward, Scott R., et al. "Analysis of Parchment Fragments from the Judean Desert Using DNA Techniques." In *Current Research & Technological Developments on the Dead Sea Scrolls*, edited by Donald W. Parry and Stephen D. Ricks, 215-238. Leiden: E. J. Brill, 1996.

## Suggestions for Further Reading: Select Recent Publications by non-Latter-day Saint Scholars

Renewed interest in the Dead Sea Scrolls has produced a plethora of publications of varying quality relating to these wonderful documents. The following short list of recent publications written by scholars for the general public contains books that we consider to be of generally high quality.

### Translations of the Dead Sea Scrolls

García Martínez, Florentino, trans. *The Dead Sea Scrolls Translated*. Translated into English by W. G. E. Watson. Leiden: E. J. Brill, 1994.

Vermes, Geza. *The Dead Sea Scrolls in English*. 4th ed. New York: Penguin, 1995.

Wise, Michael, Martin Abegg Jr., and Edward Cook. *The Dead Sea Scrolls: A New Translation*. San Francisco: Harper, 1996.

## Introductions to Qumran and the Scrolls

Cross, Frank M. *The Ancient Library of Qumran.* 3rd ed. Minneapolis: Fortress, 1995.

Fitzmyer, Joseph A. *Responses to 101 Questions on the Dead Sea Scrolls.* New York: Paulist, 1992.

Schiffman, Lawrence H. *Reclaiming the Dead Sea Scrolls.* Philadelphia: Jewish Publication Society, 1994.

VanderKam, James C. *The Dead Sea Scrolls Today.* Grand Rapids, Mich.: Eerdmans, 1994.

## Related Studies of Potential Interest

Collins, John J. *The Scepter and the Star: The Messiahs of the Dead Sea Scrolls and Other Ancient Literature.* New York: Doubleday, 1995.

Scanlin, Harold. *The Dead Sea Scrolls and Modern Translations of the Old Testament.* Wheaton, Ill.: Tyndale House, 1993.

# Acknowledgments

As the editors of this volume, we acknowledge the work of numerous individuals who assisted us in both the organization of the conference and the preparation of this volume. We appreciate the support and direction of Robert L. Millet, dean of religious education at BYU, and Noel B. Reynolds, president of FARMS. We are grateful to Brent Hall, FARMS director of operations and development, Margene Jolley, assistant to the director, others on the FARMS staff, and to Becky Schulties, a BYU graduate student in Near Eastern studies, for taking care of the numerous details involved in the planning of the conference. We express our thanks to Erik Swanson for assistance in gathering and organizing data for this introductory material. We also thank Sandra A. Thorne and Mary Mahan, the FARMS editors assigned to this volume, for their careful and accurate work.

Donald W. Parry

Dana M. Pike

## Notes

1. See Florentino García Martínez, trans., *The Dead Sea Scrolls Translated,* translated into English by Wilfred G. E. Watson (Leiden: E. J. Brill, 1994), xxvi.

2. An adaptation and expansion of points made by Noel B. Reynolds, "From the Caves of Qumran to CD-ROM," *Brigham Young Magazine* 50/4 (1996): 44–52.

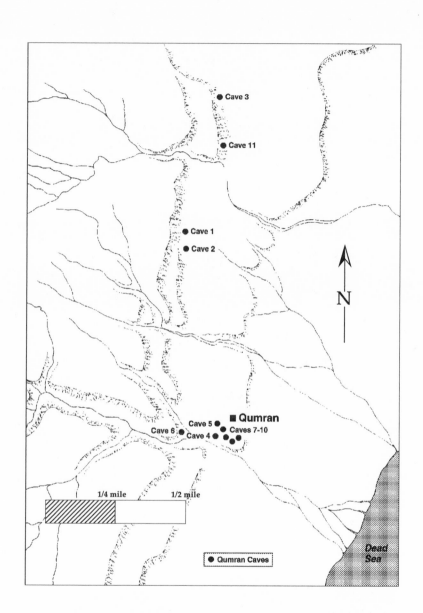

Map of the eleven Qumran caves in which the Dead Sea Scrolls were discovered. (Map by Jeff Jolley.)

CHAPTER 1

# THE ANCIENT PEOPLE OF QUMRAN:
# AN INTRODUCTION TO THE
# DEAD SEA SCROLLS

*Andrew C. Skinner*

The most fascinating thing about the Dead Sea Scrolls is the ancient people who used them. Certainly a study of the ideas found within the documents is interesting, but contemplation of the fact that those ideas actually constituted the belief system of real, live, flesh-and-blood human beings who lived some two thousand years ago on the edge of a lifeless sea is truly arresting. It is understandable that Latter-day Saints would be especially drawn to a group in the Middle East who claimed to be the true Israel and went off by themselves to establish a religiously based covenant community in desert country right next to a vast salt lake fed by a freshwater stream named the Jordan. Who those ancient people were, how they lived, where they came from, what they thought, why they thought it, what happened to them, and how we know about them are among the most profitable questions we can explore.

*Andrew C. Skinner is associate professor of ancient scripture at Brigham Young University.*

## New Documents from the Earth

The ruins of the Dead Sea Scrolls community lie on a marl terrace between limestone cliffs where a dry stream bed (called a *wadi* in Arabic) cuts a deep gorge through the ground to the Dead Sea. The Arab Bedouin call the site Khirbet Qumran or the "ruin" of Qumran (*khirbeh* in Arabic means "ruin" and Qumran is the proper name of the wadi). It is likely that the Dead Sea Scrolls community was built on an older biblical site, which several scholars equate with one of the Judean desert fortress towns called *ʿir ha-melaḥ*, "City of the Salt [Sea]" listed in Joshua 15:61–2.[1]

It should hardly be surprising to Latter-day Saints that previously unknown ancient texts, long buried in the ground, were discovered at Qumran in the middle part of the twentieth century. Joseph Smith's experience gave us a pattern of how new things might come forth from the ground, preserved from a previous age (see Joseph Smith—History 1:51–2). Restoration scripture not only speaks of God sending forth truth (the Book of Mormon) out of the earth (see Moses 7:62), but it has primed us to expect additional ancient records—both biblical and nonbiblical—"springing from the ground," to quote Psalms 85:11.

Indeed, new texts were literally taken from the earth again in 1947 near the shores of the Dead Sea, but not without some foreshadowing. Less than 250 years after Christ, the great biblical scholar Origen (A.D. 185–254) mentioned the discovery of Hebrew and Greek biblical manuscripts stored in jars in the vicinity of Jericho. The church historian Eusebius (ca. A.D. 260–340) also noted that a Greek version of the Psalms, as well as other manuscripts, had been found in a jar at Jericho during the reign of the Roman emperor Antonius son of Severus (A.D. 198–217).[2]

About five hundred years later, the Nestorian Patriarch

of Seleucia, Timotheus I, wrote a letter to Sergius, Metropolitan of Elam, in which he described the discovery of a large cache of Hebrew manuscripts in a cave near Jericho. The story of this find as described in the letter bears a striking resemblance to the account of the discoveries of 1947: when a Bedouin hunter's dog failed to emerge from a cave, the owner went in after it and found a cache of documents, both biblical and nonbiblical.[3]

No one knows for sure whether that cave was directly related to the Qumran community, but it seems more than possible when one considers other Jewish and Islamic sources. The medieval Jewish Karaite writer Kirkisani, in a history of Jewish sects written around A.D. 937, speaks of a sect called *al-Maghariya,* "the cave people," already extinct at that time. They were so called because their books were deposited in caves. According to a Muslim writer named Shahrastani, these cave people flourished around the middle of the first century A.D.[4]

No manuscript discoveries near the Dead Sea are recorded between the years 800 and 1947. However, in the spring of the latter, according to one version of the story, three Bedouin shepherds from the Ta'amireh tribe were tending their flocks at the wadi Qumran. One of them, Jum'a Muhammad Khalil, threw a rock into one of the numerous caves in the region, ostensibly to chase out a wandering goat, and shattered something in the darkness (later found to be a clay jar).

The noise frightened the shepherds away, but a couple of days later one of the shepherds, Muhammad ed-Dhib ("Muhammad the Wolf"), returned to the cave by himself and found ten jars, each about two feet in height. All but two of the jars proved to be empty. However, one yielded three parchment scrolls; two wrapped in linen and one unwrapped. These were later identified as a copy of the biblical book of Isaiah; a copy of the *Rule of the Community*, sometimes called the *Manual of Discipline* (a text outlining the rules by which the Dead Sea community was to be governed); and a commentary on the biblical book of Habakkuk. Four additional scrolls were later found in the cave: a collection of psalms or hymns known as the *Thanksgiving Hymns* or the *Hymn Scroll* (Hebrew, *Hodayot*); a partially preserved copy of Isaiah; the *War Scroll*—a text describing a final war in the last days between the Sons of Light (the righteous) and the Sons of Darkness (the wicked); and a collection of Genesis narratives called the *Genesis Apocryphon*.

The scrolls were brought to Bethlehem and placed in the custody of an antiquities dealer named Kando, who in turn sold four of them to Athanasius Yeshua Samuel, the Metropolitan, or head, of the Syrian Orthodox Church at St. Mark's Monastery in Jerusalem. For the equivalent of about one hundred dollars, Metropolitan Samuel received the more complete *Isaiah Scroll*, the *Rule of the Community*, the *Habakkuk Commentary*, and the *Genesis Apocryphon*.

Since no one really understood much about the nature or origins of the scrolls, several scholars were consulted. One of them was Eleazar Sukenik of the Hebrew University in Jerusalem. After a secret visit to the antiquities dealer on 29 November 1947 (the very date on which the United Nations passed the resolution to establish the State of Israel), Sukenik purchased the remaining three scrolls from Kando. Professor Sukenik seems to have been the first to recognize the antiquity and value of the scrolls and the first to suggest what has proved to be the most widely accepted view regarding their provenance or origin. Unfortunately, detailed study of the archaeological and historical context of the scrolls, as well as any search for more caves and scrolls, was hampered by the Arab-Israeli conflict, which was at its height.

By this time scholars connected with the American School of Oriental Research in Jerusalem also recognized the significance of the scrolls, or at least the four that Metropolitan Samuel had shown to them. They felt it was time to announce to the world the amazing find. On 11 April 1948 the American School issued a press release announcing the discovery of the St. Mark's collection. Two weeks later, Professor Sukenik announced the existence of the scrolls he had purchased. So secretive had been all the dealings surrounding both sets of scrolls from the same cave that the American School had no previous knowledge of the existence of Sukenik's scrolls.[5]

Looking back on the story of the scrolls up to that point (1948–49), one recognizes that the drama and intrigue were only just beginning! Because of the War of Independence, in 1948 Metropolitan Samuel moved his scrolls to Lebanon for safety's sake. By 1954 he had brought them to the United States in order to find a buyer. It was there that his now-famous, comically understated advertisement appeared in the June 1 issue of the *Wall Street Journal* under the category "Miscellaneous for Sale":

> THE FOUR DEAD SEA SCROLLS Biblical Manuscripts dating back to at least 200 B.C. are for sale. This would be an ideal gift to an educational or religious institution by an individual or group. Box F 206, The Wall Street Journal.[6]

The newspaper ad came to the attention of Israeli archaeologist Yigael Yadin, who, purely by coincidence, was in the United States on a speaking tour. He also happened to be the son of Professor E. L. Sukenik, who had purchased the first three scrolls in 1947. (Given these "coincidences," some may wonder if divine providence was involved.)

Through a series of cloak-and-dagger twists and turns, Yadin clandestinely negotiated for the purchase of the scrolls on behalf of the State of Israel. Yadin believed that any mention of Israel or an Israeli as the interested party would have forced Metropolitan Samuel to cancel the deal. The Kingdom of Jordan had claimed legal title to antiquities found in what was then its territory and probably would have sued any buyer—any buyer, that is, except Israel, because to do so would have implied recognition of the new state. The deal went through, and the agreed-upon purchase price of $250,000 was met.[7] The four scrolls from St. Mark's Monastery were put with Professor Sukenik's three. Adjacent to the Israel Museum, a special museum called the Shrine of the Book was constructed in West Jerusalem to house the scrolls, and that is where the original seven scrolls from Cave 1 remain to this day. Much to the credit of the early team of scholars, the contents of all seven manuscripts were translated and published by 1956.[8] They continue to provide insights into the nature and operation of the extinct community that deposited them where they were found in 1947, as well as valuable information about

The Shrine of the Book in Jerusalem, which houses several major scrolls. (Photograph courtesy Steven W. Booras.)

Second Temple Judaism and the religious environment that gave rise to Christianity.

Some of the scrolls were discovered in jars like this one, which was found at Qumran. (Photograph by David Hawkinson, courtesy the Church of Jesus Christ of Latter-day Saints and Brigham Young University, Museum of Art.)

## The Qumran Complex

Within a short time after the original announcements of the discovery of the scrolls, worldwide scholarly interest in them began to grow. The first archaeological excavation of Cave 1 was carried out between February and March 1949 by G. Lankester Harding, Director of the Department of Antiquities of the Kingdom of Jordan, and Father Roland de Vaux, distinguished biblical scholar, archaeologist, and Director of the Ecole Biblique (a degree-granting French Dominican school in Jerusalem). Artifacts and fragments of seventy-two additional manuscripts were uncovered. These fragments have also been published, bringing to seventy-nine the total number of texts from Cave 1 that have been found and analyzed.[9]

Scholars working on the site initially thought that ruins about a half mile to the south of the cave were part of an old Roman fort that had no connection to the manuscripts. But in the early 1950s, scholarly debate grew more intense, prompting a decision by archaeologists to conduct a full-scale excavation of the area and rethink their conclusions.

Between 1951 and 1956, Khirbet Qumran was excavated and partially restored. Father de Vaux was able to discern that the Qumran complex had been built around 150 B.C. and was inhabited until A.D. 68. He believed that a thirty-one-year gap in occupation occurred immediately following the great Near Eastern earthquake of 31 B.C. The community was apparently attacked and destroyed about A.D. 68 by Roman soldiers who came to Palestine to put down the First Jewish Revolt (A.D. 66–74). Soldiers were garrisoned there well past the fall of Masada in A.D. 74.

The Qumran complex appears to have been the religious center for a communal society of Jews living in the area. Archaeological evidence indicates that the people actually lived outside the building complex in tents, huts, or, most likely, the more than two hundred caves and underground chambers in the hills west of the complex. The complex was built of stone and included a seventy-five-foot-long refectory, or dining hall, used for meals and assembly. Excavation of an adjoining pantry yielded over one thousand bowls, plates, beakers, and assorted other vessels.[10]

The most distinctive feature of the Qumran complex is its gravity-flow aqueduct system, which brought water from the nearby cliffs and was interconnected to a series of cisterns, ritual baths, and a decantation pool. This was an exceptional hydrological engineering feat, and such emphasis on fresh water was more than just a reaction to the desert environment. The members of the community had to purify themselves by bathing in fresh water before entering the "holy temple" (sacred area) of the refectory to partake of the communal meal.[11]

Also of special interest at Qumran are the remains of a chamber some scholars labeled the Scriptorium, or "writing room." According to the theory first proposed by de Vaux, here the community scribes copied many of the scrolls that were later found in the nearby caves. He reached his conclusion on the basis of inkwells found there as well as installations he thought were desks. An alternate theory that has gained adherents is championed by a Belgian team of archaeologists, Robert Donceel and his wife, Pauline Donceel-Voûte, hired by the Ecole Biblique to complete the unfinished final excavation report of de Vaux. Based on the conclusions of earlier scholars who disagreed with de Vaux regarding the existence of a Scriptorium, the Donceels interpret the evidence as pointing to the existence of a *coenaculum* or a *triclinium*—another dining room (de Vaux had already found the large refectory) to be used for a small number of guests who took their meals in typical Hellenistic fashion, reclining on couches. Others have even suggested more recently that Qumran was "but a customs post, entrepôt for goods and a resting stop for travelers crossing the Salt Sea."[12]

De Vaux's idea that writing desks existed at Qumran has now been abandoned by some scholars because there is no evidence that ancient writers of the period used desks. De Vaux himself was aware of this, but the discovery of inkwells at Locus 30 (the site of de Vaux's proposed Scriptorium) is problematic in any interpretation that attempts to posit a triclinium there. The former curator of the Shrine of the Book and expert on the Qumran site, Magen Broshi, says that in the final analysis, there is "a high probability the room was a Scriptorium."[13] The assertion that Qumran was not a religious settlement that produced the documents found in nearby caves also becomes very tenuous when considered in light of evidence uncovered in 1992. Professor Shemaryahu Talmon of the Hebrew University in Jerusalem explains:

> The connection of the caves with the ancient settlement was conclusively proven in the winter of 1992. Exceptionally heavy rainfalls eroded a sand wall on the site and laid bare a completely preserved, albeit empty, earthenware jar of exactly the same make as the intact jar found in Cave 1 which had served as the receptacle of the four scrolls.[14]

After excavating the Qumran complex of buildings, archaeologists turned their attention to locating more caves and more scrolls. It was the Ta'amireh Bedouin, however, who proved to be more adept at making new discoveries. Between 1952 and 1956, ten more caves containing manuscripts were found at Qumran, making eleven caves in all that yielded texts. The Bedouin are credited with having discovered the richest repositories of documents—Caves 1, 2, 4, and 11, while professional archaeologists located Caves 3, 5, 7, 8, 9, and 10—none of which contained impressive numbers of manuscripts.[15] To date, the total number of separate documents recovered from all eleven caves is 818.[16]

The Bedouin also discovered some manuscript fragments in caves in the remote Wadi Murabba'at region, about twelve miles south of Qumran, and in the Nahal Hever caves, which lie just past Ein Gedi. These fragments include a variety of papyrus and sheepskin documents dating from the second century A.D., as well as coins from the Second Jewish, or Bar Kokhba, Revolt (A.D. 132–35). There were also biblical manuscripts closely related to the Masoretic Text of the Old Testament (the text type from which our King James Version was translated in the early seventeenth century). The two most important documents found were a fragmentary copy of the Hebrew text of ten of the minor prophets (Joel through Zechariah), and a fragmentary copy of the Greek translation of six of the minor prophets.[17] More significant from a historical point of view was the discovery of original letters from Simeon ben Kosiba (nicknamed Bar Kokhba), the actual leader of the Second Jewish Revolt. These letters lent a dramatic air to the finds.[18]

The overall importance of the manuscripts and artifacts found in the region south of Qumran is twofold. First, they show that many refugees fled from Roman troops who occupied the area. Second, they bear witness to the "trilingualism that prevailed at this time in Judea, showing that Aramaic, Greek, and Hebrew were all being used by the people who took refuge in these caves from the Romans."[19]

The greatest treasure trove of documents in the entire Dead Sea region came from Qumran Cave 4, a bell-shaped underground dwelling artificially enlarged by community dwellers that was situated closest to the Qumran buildings. Of the fragments of 584 manuscripts recovered from Cave 4 (literally 40,000 separate scraps or pieces[20]), 127 appear to be biblical texts. Every book of the Old Testament except Esther is represented. In addition, two other categories of documents were found: those that are called apocryphal or pseudepigraphical texts, and those that may be termed "indigenous" documents (sometimes called sectarian documents), which are scripturelike texts used primarily or exclusively at Qumran.

The indigenous documents are of special importance because, when put with the documents from Cave 1, they show the nature of the Qumran covenanters' conceptual universe and the socioreligious structure of their community. These documents (what Professor Shemaryahu

Talmon calls the "Foundation Documents"[21]) help define the unique nature and outlook of the Qumran community. On the other hand, the apocryphal and pseudepigraphical books found at Qumran are interesting, but are not as helpful for understanding what is different about the people of Qumran because they have been found in other places. They bear such titles as the *Testaments of the Twelve Patriarchs*, Tobit, *Jubilees*, and *1 Enoch*, and were known in normative or Pharisaic Judaism of the first centuries B.C. and A.D., though generally they were not highly regarded. Some early Christians, however, used Greek and Ethiopic versions of these and other apocryphal books and included them in their biblical canon.

Besides the documents of Cave 4, the most intriguing texts were found in Cave 3 (discovered in 1953) and Cave 11 (discovered in 1956). Cave 3, the first to be discovered by professional archaeologists, contained the famous *Copper Scroll*—a description of buried treasure that was written on a thin metal scroll (the ancients really did write on metal plates!). The *Copper Scroll* is now housed in the Amman Archaeological Museum, and although people have looked carefully no one has found any of the treasure.

Last but not least, Cave 11 yielded the longest of all the scrolls—the *Temple Scroll*. Written on very thin parchment, the text disclosed two different scribal hands and turned out to be about twenty-seven feet long, although not intact (the great *Isaiah Scroll* from Cave 1 is twenty-two feet long and is intact). Dating to about the second century before Christ but presented as the words of God to Moses, the text of the *Temple Scroll* supplies laws dealing with issues important to the Qumran group. Of interest to Latter-day Saints is the scroll's description of an ideal temple to be established by God himself at the end of days, and that temple's association with Jacob at Bethel. The *Temple Scroll* states:

And I will consecrate my Temple by my glory, [the Temple] on which I will settle my glory, until the day of the blessing [or, the day of creation] on which I will create my Temple and establish it for myself for all times, according to the Covenant which I have made with Jacob at Bethel.[22]

While Latter-day Saints might remember that President Marion G. Romney called the events at Bethel "Jacob's endowment experience,"[23] we have no indication that the Qumran community regarded this ideal future temple as anything more than an Aaronic priesthood structure, associated with the rites and rituals of the Mosaic Law in a pure and uncorrupted form. The Qumran community believed that the Jerusalem Temple was full of corruption.[24]

## Identity and History of the Qumran People

Following the suggestion of Eleazar Sukenik,[25] Frank Moore Cross of Harvard University, one of the original scholars of the scrolls, definitively and succinctly identified the inhabitants of the ancient Dead Sea Scroll community of Qumran as Essenes.[26] The Essenes were one of the four Jewish "philosophies," or sects, described by the first-century historian Josephus as the major competing ideologies contemporary in the Holy Land.

More recently Professor Cross reemphasized the Qumran-Essene connection by reminding us that a scholar who would suggest any non-Essene identification for the Dead Sea Scroll community "places himself in an astonishing position."[27] For, in essence, one must explain away the simplest and most logical interpretations of historical sources in favor of more complicated theories based on supposition and inference. Professor Cross states:

He [the scholar] must seriously suggest that *two* major

parties formed communalistic religious communities in the same district of the Dead Sea and lived together in effect for two centuries, holding similar bizarre views, performing similar or rather identical lustrations, ritual meals, and ceremonies. He must suppose that one, carefully described by classical authors, disappeared without leaving building remains or even potsherds behind; the other, systematically ignored by the classical sources, left extensive ruins, and indeed a great library. I prefer to be reckless and flatly identify the men of Qumran with their perennial house guests, the Essenes.[28]

Unfortunately, none of the Dead Sea Scrolls comes right out and explicitly states, "We are Essenes!" (though one gets the impression that such a declaration still might not be conclusive enough for some scholars). One of the most significant recent challenges to the Essene theory of Qumran identity was put forward by a scholar whose opinions carry significant weight, Lawrence Schiffman of New York University. He claims that the community members were Sadducees. This is based on similarities between legal issues found in a recently published Qumran text called *Miqsat Maʿaseh ha-Torah* (4QMMT) and certain legal positions that the Mishnah attributes to the Sadducees.

But the basic argument really seems to be one of semantics rather than substance, because Schiffman says that the Sadducees he is championing are not the aristocratic sect described by Josephus and the New Testament, but rather a different group, one that was conservative in its approach to the law and whose name also derives from "Zadok," just like the more famous group. This is not very helpful or insightful information because we already knew from Qumran texts that the leaders at Qumran called *themselves* the Sons of Zadok, and that their orientation and outlook was priestly.[29] In addition, Schiffman overlooks many

Qumran texts that express non-Sadducean theological concepts, ideas that better fit within an Essene context.[30] Hence, the view expressed so eloquently by Professor Cross continues to be the most widely held position.

## History of the Community

No single document found at Qumran, or elsewhere for that matter, constitutes anything like a purposeful history of the sect. However, from classical sources, archaeological evidence, and passages within the scrolls themselves, one can glean enough clues to put together a historical sketch of the community.

Both Josephus and Philo indicate that the total number of Essenes in the Holy Land was about four thousand. But archaeologists and historians estimate the number of persons living at the Dead Sea community at any one time to have been between 150 and 300. This indicates that the Essenes residing at Qumran were a very small part of the larger Essene movement in the ancient Near East.

Of the various ideas scholars have proposed regarding the origin of the Essenes, two basic theories have endured. One theory traces the beginnings of the sect to the exiled Jews living in Babylonia (587–538 B.C.). According to this scenario many of the Jewish deportees perceived the Babylonian captivity as divine retribution for unrighteousness. In response they bound themselves together as a covenant group devoted to the perfect observance of the law. Some of the group returned to the Holy Land at a time when Maccabean Jewish victories over the Greek Syrians (the Seleucids) seemed to ensure the renewal of an independent Jewish state (sometime between 165 and 143 B.C.).

Once they arrived back in Palestine, however, they became bitterly disappointed and disillusioned over the extreme Hellenization of Judaism that controlled the state. After an unsuccessful attempt to return their erring brethren to the truth, the covenantors retreated to the isolation of Qumran on the shores of the Dead Sea. Rallying behind a leader referred to in their documents as the Teacher of Righteousness, the group adhered to their strict lifestyle, believing that their divinely revealed precepts constituted the only sure refuge against the imminent judgments of a messianic age.

The other and perhaps more commonly accepted theory suggests that the Essenes originated in Palestine during the period of Hellenization. Advocates of this theory refer to certain passages of the *Damascus Document*—a document of commandments and exhortations that has been known since medieval times.[31] In the *Damascus Document*, the birth of the community is said to have occurred in the "age of wrath," 390 years after the destruction of Jerusalem by Nebuchadnezzar of Babylon. At that time God caused a "root" to spring "from Israel and Aaron." In other words, a group of righteous Jews encountered apostate conditions and formed a company of dissenters. They groped in darkness for twenty years until God sent them the famed Teacher of Righteousness (sometimes translated the "teacher who is right"), and he guided them "in the way of [God's] heart."[32] Nebuchadnezzar razed Jerusalem and its temple in 587 B.C. Subtracting the years mentioned in the *Damascus Document* (390 years after Jerusalem's destruction, plus the other 20 years that were filled with struggle) places the founding of the community at approximately 177 B.C.

But, say the texts, things were not immediately and universally harmonious among the Jewish reformers. Conflicts between the Teacher and others seem to have arisen, and understandably so when one considers the force of the

Teacher's claims that God specifically revealed to him all the mysteries of the prophets.[33] Some are said to have turned against him and formed a breakaway group. They persecuted the Teacher and his disciples who withdrew to the "land of Damascus" (Qumran?) where they entered into a new covenant. The leader of the dissenters is branded as the "Scoffer" and the "Man of Lies" (one who led many astray through deceptive speech) in the words of the *Damascus Document* and some of the community's scriptural commentaries.[34] This certainly sounds familiar to readers of latter-day revelation—similar occurrences are described in Alma 30 and Moses 4. The *Commentary on Psalm 37* found at Qumran states explicitly that the Teacher of Righteousness was a priest. His primary contemporary opponent is called "the Wicked Priest" (Hebrew, *ha-kohen ha-rasha*) in several Qumran texts. Scholars believe that the epithet is a play on words alluding to the Jerusalem high priest, who was called in Hebrew *ha-kohen ha-ro'sh*[35] and was the man who was perceived by the Essenes as the enemy of all righteousness.

This theory of the Essene origins, including consideration of the dates provided in the *Damascus Document*, seems to accord well with what is known of the history of the second century B.C. The historical details of the period are outlined in the apocryphal books of First and Second Maccabees. According to those records, the process of Hellenization in the Holy Land began almost imperceptibly in the third century B.C. In the first part of the second century B.C., however, the forces of Hellenization gained new ground. In 172 B.C., Onias III, the legitimate high priest, was murdered in Jerusalem. Onias was a Zadokite, a priest who was descended from Zadok (King David's high priest and the originator of the line of high priests at the Temple of Jerusalem). In place of Onias, the Syrian rulers of the region appointed Meneleus, an intensely Hellenized Jew not of the Zadokite line. To the faithful, Meneleus was a usurper.

Matters went from bad to worse when the Syrian over-lord, King Antiochus IV, forced Judeans to Hellenize upon penalty of death. In 168 B.C. Judea revolted. Under the brilliant military leadership of Judah the Maccabee, the revolt was successful, and an independent Jewish state was once again established. This victory is still celebrated by Jews in the festival of Hanukkah. The Hasmonean line of Jewish rulers began with these events. Judah the Maccabee was first recognized as unofficial monarch (165–160 B.C.), followed by his brother Jonathan (160–143 B.C.). As it turned out, however, the latter began to dismiss orthodoxy and increase Hellenization.

Two events marked the culmination of degradation. The first came in 152 B.C. when Jonathan had himself appointed High Priest. This act was the ultimate provocation for many Jews and gave them a strong reason for abhorring the Hasmoneans. But the second event was far more significant. In 141 B.C. Simon (143–134 B.C.), the youngest surviving brother of Judah and Jonathan, accepted both the high priesthood and the official title of king. The high priesthood of the Aaronic order was now made hereditary in the Hasmonean line, and an independent Jewish state emerged in which the civil head and military leader of the state was at the same time high priest. A decree was issued that warned against any opposition to Simon by priest or layman alike, and prohibited private assembly or any other actions deemed contrary to the stipulations of the decree.

It was in this atmosphere that the Essene movement began, according to several scholars. Some Jews, disgusted by what they believed was the pollution of their ancestral religion and the usurpation of the high priesthood by non-Zadokites, rallied behind their Moreh Tzedek, the Teacher

Professor Andrew C. Skinner studying scroll fragments in Jerusalem's Rockefeller Museum.

of Righteousness.[36] While no clues disclose the identity of the Teacher of Righteousness (it most assuredly cannot be Jesus or John the Baptist), Professor Cross argues that we probably can deduce the identity of the Wicked Priest— Simon the Hasmonean. Simon's program of absolute control "seems to give the appropriate occasion for the crystallization of the Essene sect."[37] In addition, a document entitled *List of Testimonia* from Cave 4 at Qumran seems to describe Ptolemy's assassination of his father-in-law, Simon, who was in a drunken stupor in Jericho. Finally, on the basis of evidence from the *Commentary on Habakkuk,* Professor Cross observes:

> In this era one cannot complain of a shortage of wicked priests. One final text, however, deserves mention. In a passage of the Commentary on Habakkuk, the expositor comments, "This means the priest whose dishonor was greater than his honor. For he . . . walked in the ways of drunkedness in order to quench his thirst. But the cup of God's wrath will swallow him up . . . !" The high priest

caroused once too often. In Jericho, at the hands of Ptolemy, the cup of pleasure turned into the cup of wrath and swallowed Simon.[38]

## Evidence from Primary Sources: Descriptions of Location

Evidence from primary sources that supports the identification of the Qumran community as an Essene center is of two types: classical sources that explicitly place Essenes on the western shore of the Dead Sea approximately near the site of Qumran, and descriptions in classical writings of the beliefs and practices of the Essenes that match those of the Qumran community as depicted in their own texts and by their artifacts.

### Pliny the Elder

The ancient Roman historian Pliny the Elder compiled a detailed list of places and curiosities throughout the Roman world from Spain to India. When describing the Dead Sea, one of the earth's marvels because it is both the lowest point on land and the saltiest body of water on the planet, he made the following observation:

> On the west side of the Dead Sea, but out of range of the noxious exhalations of the coast, is the solitary tribe of the Essenes [Esseni], which is remarkable beyond all other tribes in the whole world, as it has renounced all sexual desire, has no money, and has only palm-trees for company. Day by day the throng of refugees is recruited to an equal number by numerous accessions of persons tired of life and driven thither by waves of fortune to adopt their manners. Thus through thousands of ages (incredible to relate) a race in which no one is born lives

on for ever; so prolific for their advantage is other men's weariness of life!

Lying below the Essenes [literally: these] was formerly the town of Engedi, second only to Jerusalem in the fertility of its land and in its groves of palm-trees but now like Jerusalem a heap of ashes.[39]

Though a few discrepancies arise when one matches the details of Pliny's description with the actual site of Khirbet Qumran,[40] resolutions of the difficulties have been presented, and his text remains one of the pillars on which the widely accepted notions of both Essene habitation of Qumran and Essene authorship of the scrolls rest.[41]

### Dio Chrysostom's Writings

The classical writer Dio Chrysostom (ca. A.D. 40–112) is also reported to have written that the Essenes were located near the Dead Sea. Chrysostom's biographer, Synesius of Cyrene (ca. A.D. 400), commented concerning some lost writings on this subject: "Also somewhere he praises the Essenes, who form an entire and prosperous city near the Dead Sea, in the centre of Palestine, not far from Sodom."[42] The significance of this comment lies in the fact that it provides us with another independent historical source that definitely identifies a Dead Sea community in the middle of Palestine as being Essene.

## Descriptions of Distinctive Beliefs and Practices

If we had only the evidence of Pliny and Dio Chrysostom at our disposal, alternate theories regarding the identity of the Qumran community would still seem inferior. In truth, however, we have much more. The second body of evidence helping to identify the Qumranites as

Essenes comes from comparisons between classical sources that describe Essene theology and the Dead Sea Scrolls themselves. The ancient writers Josephus (A.D. 38–100), Pliny (A.D. 23–79), Philo Judaeus (ca. 20 B.C.–A.D. 50), and Hippolytus (A.D. 170–235) complement and agree with the Qumran texts to an impressive degree. One scholar compared descriptions of beliefs and practices from Josephus and from the scrolls and concluded that there are twenty-seven definite parallels between Josephus and the scrolls; twenty-one probable parallels; ten concepts in Josephus that have no known parallels in the scrolls; and six apparent discrepancies between the two sources regarding beliefs or practices of the Essenes versus Qumranites.[43] This impressive tally has been increased by other experts who have explained and harmonized many of the difficulties between Josephus and the scrolls.[44]

Following are the most significant parallels documented by both the major classical authors and the scrolls that help identify the ancient people of Qumran as Essenes.

### Common Ownership of Property

A seminal point on which the scrolls and classical descriptions of the Essenes coincide regards the individual ownership of property. Both the Jewish philosopher Philo and the Jewish historian Josephus speak in admiring tones about common ownership of property among the Essenes. From Josephus's *Jewish War* we read:

> Riches they despise, and their community of goods is truly admirable; you will not find one among them distinguished by greater opulence than another. They have a law that new members on admission to the sect shall confiscate their property to the order, with the result that you will nowhere see either abject poverty or inordinate

wealth; the individual's possessions join the common stock and all, like brothers, enjoy a single patrimony.[45]

The Qumran text entitled the *Rule of the Community* lays out the legal principles by which property is regulated among members of the covenant community:

> Then when he has completed one year within the Community, the Congregation shall deliberate his case with regard to his understanding and observance of the Law. And if it be his destiny, according to the judgement of the Priests and the multitude of the men of their Covenant, to enter the company of the Community, his property and earnings shall be handed over to the Bursar of the Congregation who shall register it to his account and shall not spend it for the Congregation. . . . But when the second year has passed, he shall be examined, and if it be his destiny, according to the judgement of the Congregation, to enter the Community, then he shall be inscribed among his brethren in the order of his rank for the Law, and for justice, and for the pure Meal; his property shall be merged and he shall offer his counsel and judgement to the Community.[46]

### Predestination

Another important identifying parallel centers on the theological concept described variously as predestination, predeterminism, or the doctrine of fate. Josephus describes the differences between the major sects of Judaism regarding this idea:

> As for the Pharisees, they say that certain events are the work of Fate, but not all; as to other events, it depends upon ourselves whether they shall take place or not. The sect of the Essenes, however, declares that Fate is mistress of all things, and that nothing befalls men unless it be in accordance with her decree. But the Sadducees do away with Fate.[47]

A parallel belief at Qumran is articulated in a number of texts, including different copies of the *Thanksgiving Scroll*, the *War Rule*, the *Damascus Document*, and the *Rule of the Community*. This quote from the *Rule of the Community* shows the Qumran parallel with Josephus's description of the Essenes. Keep in mind that Josephus wrote for gentile readers, and that members of the Jewish sects would have discussed the notion of God's predetermined plan instead of "Fate":

> From the God of Knowledge comes all that is and shall be. Before ever they existed He established their whole design, and when, as ordained for them, they come into being, it is in accord with His glorious design that they accomplish their task without change.[48]

Also instructive are a few lines from a Qumran text called the *Ages of the Creation* (4Q180):[49] "Interpretation concerning the ages made by God, all the ages for the accomplishment [of all the events, past] and future. Before ever He created them, He determined the works of . . . age by age."[50]

## The Afterlife

The few Old Testament references to an afterlife are expanded in nonbiblical texts found at Qumran. The book of *Jubilees* (not original to Qumran but probably regarded as canonical scripture there)[51] gives perhaps the best representation of the Qumran idea of life beyond mortality:

> Then the Lord will heal his servants. They will rise and see great peace. He will expel their enemies. The righteous will see (this), offer praise, and be very happy forever and ever. They will see all their punishments and curses on their enemies. Their bones will rest in the earth and their spirits will be very happy. They will know that

> the Lord is the one who executes judgment but shows
> kindness to hundreds and thousands and to all who love
> him.[52]

This text indicates that a fundamental aspect of the belief
in an afterlife at Qumran was centered on an assurance
of the immortality of the soul and continued existence
with the angels of heaven, but without benefit of a bodily
resurrection.

The nature of the afterlife described in texts from
Qumran matches closely Josephus's understanding of the
basic Essene belief in the immortality of the soul. In fact,
Josephus draws important distinctions between the Essenes
and the Pharisees, as well as between the Essenes and the
Sadducees. The Pharisees believed in a bodily resurrection
in addition to believing in the everlasting nature of the soul.
The Sadducees denied the idea of the immortality of both
body and soul. Of the Essenes Josephus says:

> It is a fixed belief of theirs that the body is corruptible and
> its constituent matter impermanent, but that the soul is
> immortal and imperishable. Emanating from the finest
> ether, these souls become entangled, as it were, in the
> prison-house of the body to which they are dragged
> down by a sort of natural spell; but once they are released
> from the bonds of the flesh, then, as though liberated
> from a long servitude, they rejoice and are borne aloft.
> Sharing the belief of the sons of Greece, they maintain
> that for virtuous souls there is reserved an abode beyond
> the ocean.[53]

Analysis of a messianic text from Qumran entitled *Messianic Apocalypse* (4Q521) indicates that at least one person
associated with the community may have also believed in a
bodily resurrection. It is not clear from the document who is
acting—God or the Messiah—but this description seems to
be a direct reference to bodily resurrection: "He will heal

the slain, and the dead he will cause to live."[54] Since most of the Qumran texts support Josephus's assertion that bodily resurrection was not taught at Qumran, this reference does not call into question an Essene identification of the Qumran community. It may, however, give some credence to the description of Hippolytus who, writing in the second century A.D., long after the physical demise of the Qumran community, said that the Essenes *did* believe in resurrection. It is possible that the perspectives presented by both Josephus and Hippolytus are valid, even though they seem to contradict one another, because their information could have come from different sources. Josephus may have presented the doctrine held by the majority, while Hippolytus's perspective might have been based on doctrines held by a few individuals.

### The Communal Meal

One of the distinctive practices of the community involved a ritual cleansing followed by the partaking of a communal meal. As noted above, archaeological evidence testifies of the importance attached to an abundant supply of fresh water at Qumran. Several passages from the *Rule of the Community* describe the meal and cleansing activity of the regular members of the covenant community:

> They shall eat in common and pray in common and deliberate in common. Wherever there are ten men of the Council of the Community there shall not lack a Priest among them. And they shall sit before him according to their rank and shall be asked their counsel in all things in that order. And when the table has been prepared for eating, and the new wine for drinking, the Priest shall be the first to stretch out his hand to bless the first-fruits of the bread and new wine.[55]

They shall not enter the water to partake of the pure Meal of the Saints, for they shall not be cleansed unless they turn from their wickedness: for all who transgress His word are unclean.[56]

After he [anyone] has entered the Council of the Community he shall not touch the pure Meal of the Congregation until one full year is completed, and until he has been examined concerning his spirit and deeds.[57]

Josephus describes similar activities among the Essenes in language that strongly links those activities to the practices of the Qumran covenanters. He says the Essenes work until the fifth hour of the day, then

they again assemble in one place and, after girding their loins with linen clothes, bathe their bodies in cold water. After this purification, they assemble in a private apartment which none of the uninitiated is permitted to enter; pure now themselves, they repair to the refectory, as to some sacred shrine. When they have taken their seats in silence, the baker serves out the loaves to them in order, and the cook sets before each one plate with a single course. Before meat the priest says grace, and none may partake until after the prayer.[58]

The fact that the *Rule of the Community* and Josephus agree on specific aspects of the communal meal—including practices not found among the members of any other known groups in the ancient world—makes identification of Qumran with the Essenes virtually certain. Both Josephus and the *Rule of the Community* describe premeal ritual bathing, the observance of a specific ranking among participants, and prohibitions against initiates partaking of the pure meal (the Qumran covenanters enforced a strict initiation procedure, requiring a mandatory two-year probationary period before applicants could become full-fledged members of the covenant community). Such evidence for Essene identification of the Qumran settlement is impressive.

## Non-Use of Oil

The curious practice among Essenes of avoiding the use of oil is described by Josephus: "Oil they consider defiling, and anyone who accidentally comes in contact with it scours his person; for they make a point of keeping a dry skin and of always being dressed in white."[59] The Qumran texts not only speak of the same practice, but actually explain why it was observed. In a text entitled *Miqsat Ma'aseh ha-Torah* (4QMMT) we learn that Qumranites believed that liquids were superconductors of ritual impurity, particularly when oil held in one container came in contact with another vessel. Hence, oil on the skin increased the danger of being contaminated by other objects carrying ritual uncleanness.[60]

## Toilet Habits

As one scholar notes, the parallels between classical sources and Qumran texts run the gamut from the lofty and sublime to the lowliest and mundane.[61] This is nowhere better demonstrated than by discussions of ancient toilet practices. Josephus reports that the Essenes did not defecate on the Sabbath:

> On other days they dig a trench a foot deep with a mattock—such is the nature of the hatchet which they present to the neophytes—and wrapping their mantle about them, that they may not offend the rays of the deity, sit above it. They then replace the excavated soil in the trench. For this purpose they select the more retired spots. And though this discharge of the excrements is a natural function, they make it a rule to wash themselves after it, as if defiled.[62]

From the *War Rule* at Qumran, a text describing regulations for the conduct of a holy war against evil in the last days, we have an exact parallel to Josephus regarding the ritually contaminating properties of bodily discharges as well as the offensiveness of nudity associated with defecation: "No man shall go down with them on the day of battle who is impure because of his 'founts,' for the holy angels shall be their hosts. And there shall be a space of about two thousand cubits between all their camps for the place serving as a latrine, so that no indecent nakedness may be seen in the surroundings of their camps."[63]

Two other bits of information are instructive. A hatchet of the type described by Josephus has apparently been found in Cave 11. And the *Temple Scroll,* also from Cave 11, offers legislation on proper toilet procedures that links the Essenes of Jerusalem with the Qumran covenanters. The *Temple Scroll,* which describes God's ideal, pure temple in the holy city of Jerusalem, states. "And you shall make them a place for a hand [latrines] outside the city to which they shall go out, to the north-west of the city—roofed houses with pits within them, into which the excrement will descend, so that it will not be visible at any distance from the city."[64]

Jacob Milgrom, an authority on ancient Israelite concepts of purity and holiness, offers this comment:

> Because of the Temple Scroll, we have the support of an outside source that, indeed, the Qumran sect was part of the Essene movement. For the law of Qumran was practiced by the Essenes of Jerusalem [toilet regulations]. Moreover, Josephus tells us that one of Jerusalem's gates was called the Essene Gate. Heretofore it has never been identified. Josephus locates it near a place called *Bethso.* That name too has never been identified. But thanks to the Temple Scroll, both problems have been solved.

> *Bethso*, it turns out, is not a place name. It is Hebrew *beth so'ah* or "toilet." Thus the Essene gate [*sic*] was not a real gate but an opening in the city wall at the nearest point to their toilets, a wicket which they could squeeze through one at a time.[65]

The Essene Gate has now been found in what was the northwest section of ancient Jerusalem.

### Spitting

The last bit of evidence we shall cite is important precisely because it is such a curious little detail. Both Josephus and the *Rule of the Community* report that spitting was prohibited among the Essenes and at Qumran. The *Rule of the Community* declares that "whosoever has spat in an Assembly of the Congregation shall do penance for thirty days."[66] Similarly, Josephus says of the Essenes, "They are careful not to spit into the midst of the company or to the right."[67]

More detailed parallels could be drawn and intricate arguments constructed. But enough of the salient features of the Qumran community have been outlined to demonstrate the weighty evidence in favor of definitively identifying the Qumran sectaries as Essenes. Let us now briefly round out our picture of life and institutions at Qumran.

## Other Practices and Parallels at Qumran

The scrolls indicate that the Qumran sectaries regarded themselves as the true Israel surrounded by spiritual traitors and false brethren in a corrupt world. A major theme of the Dead Sea Scrolls concerns the members of the Qumran community awaiting the advent of certain messiahs from their wilderness habitation, where apostasy and persecution had driven them. A similar idea appears in Revelation 12:1–6, which describes a celestial woman giving birth to a son, who is caught into heaven to be preserved, while she (the true church or congregation of the righteous) flees to the wilderness because of intense apostasy and persecution. She was to come forth in a later time of refreshing (see also Acts 3:19–21).

Qumran texts clearly attest a form of messianic belief, as do other pre-Christian Israelite writings. The Qumran documents indicate that the community lived in expectation of a coming prophet (probably the one promised to Moses in Deuteronomy 18:18: "I will raise them up a Prophet from among their brethren, like unto thee, and will put my words in his mouth") who would precede the Anointed One. And instead of one messiah, Qumran texts disclose the anticipation of two: a priestly Anointed One (the Messiah of Aaron), and a Davidic, political Anointed One (the Messiah of Israel). While the Mosaic law was basically an interim covenant that the community members were obligated to observe with exactitude because it was designed to keep God's people spiritually safe during the great age of wrath or wickedness, the advent of the Messiahs would usher in a new era of Mosaic purity, peace, and pardon. From the *Rule of the Community* and the *Damascus Document* we read:

> They shall depart from no counsel of the Law to walk in all the stubbornness of their hearts, but they shall be governed by the primitive precepts in which the men of the community were first instructed, until the coming of a prophet and the Messiahs of Aaron and Israel.[68]

> This is the exact statement of the statutes in which [they shall walk until the coming of the Messia]h of Aaron and Israel who will pardon their iniquity.[69]

Believing they were God's true Israel, the community organized their movement to correspond to biblical Israel, dividing members into priests and laity: the priests being described as the "sons of Zadok" (Zadok was high priest in king David's time) and the laity grouped into twelve tribes. In describing true and proper temple worship, the *War Rule* says:

> And the twelve chief Priests shall minister at the daily sacrifice before God. . . . Below them . . . shall be the chiefs of the Levites to the number of twelve, one for each tribe. . . . Below them shall be the chiefs of the tribes.[70]

The Qumran covenanters viewed their community or congregation (*yaḥad* in Hebrew) as a link in the historical chain that snapped when Judah was conquered by the Babylonians. This self-identification as the sole legitimate representative of biblical Israel distinguishes the community from their opponents, who regarded the biblical period as a closed chapter, and their authorities—the rabbis—as leading a new phase in the history of Israel.[71]

Thus the *yaḥad* held in high regard the prophets, prophetic teaching, and divine revelation manifested in the Bible. Almost from the start, the community subjected itself to the guidance of men believed to be gifted with the holy spirit. The first to appear among the people was the Teacher of Righteousness, as earlier noted. Because they were considered divinely inspired, the Teacher's decisions were beyond debate and unconditionally binding on the members of community.[72]

After the passing of the Teacher of Righteousness, the primary leadership of the Dead Sea community was vested in a governing quorum of three priests who worked in tandem with a quorum of twelve laymen, all possessing the divine spirit:

In the deliberative council of the community there shall be twelve laymen and three priests schooled to perfection in all that has been revealed of the entire Law. Their duty shall be to set the standard for the practice of truth, righteousness and justice, and for the exercise of charity and humility in human relations; ... So long as these men exist in Israel, the deliberative council of the community will rest securely on a basis of truth.[73]

One is immediately reminded of the Quorum of Twelve Apostles in first-century Christianity, and its three chief leaders, Peter, James, and John (although the latter do not appear to have functioned as a separate entity outside of the Twelve). Qumran also had an officer called an overseer, who seems to have held a position almost the equivalent to that of bishop in the early Christian church (the Greek word *episcopos,* translated as "bishop," literally means "overseer.") Temporal and practical matters were the responsibility of the overseer at Qumran, as they were in the Christian bishop's role (see 1 Timothy 3:1–7; Titus 1:7–9; and even Acts 6:1–3).

However, the important point here is that the influence of the holy spirit was emphasized among both Christians and Qumran covenanters. By contrast, as Professor Talmon points out, rabbinic Judaism, which developed alongside these other two branches of Judaism, progressively moved away from prophets and "the spirit," and developed a rationalist stance. According to rabbinic tradition, after the demise of the last biblical prophets—Haggai, Zechariah, and Malachi—"the holy spirit departed from Israel," and from then on Israel was enjoined to incline their ear and "listen to the instructions of the [rabbinic] Sages."[74]

Given the biblically based environment at Qumran, and the historically connected consciousness among the people, it is not surprising that the covenanters applied the term

*Renewed Covenant* to the totality of laws and principles to which they strictly adhered. Basing his analysis on the *Damascus Document* (abbreviated CD), Professor Talmon summarizes the views of the Qumran covenanters:

> They view[ed] their community as the youngest link in a chain of sequential reaffirmations of the covenant, to which the Bible gives witness (CD II,14–III, 20). God had originally established his covenant with Adam. He renewed it after each critical juncture in the history of the world, and of Israel; after the flood, with Noah, the 'second Adam'; then with the patriarchs; again with all Israel at Sinai; with the priestly house of Aaron; and ensuingly with the royal house of David, after the monarchical system had taken root in Israel. In the present generation . . . "he raised for himself" from among all evildoers "men called by name, that a remnant be left in the land, and that the earth be filled with their offspring" (CD II, 11–12). The thread of Israel's historical past, which snapped when Jerusalem and the temple were destroyed, is retied with the foundation of the *yaḥad*'s 'renewed covenant.'[75]

Though grounded in the Bible, it is not exactly certain how the Qumran Essenes viewed marriage because their texts do not speak of it. Excavations of the large main cemetery, fifty meters east of the community ruins, plus excavations of two secondary cemeteries carried out by de Vaux in the 1950s present an inconclusive picture. The majority of the skeletons were male, but women and children have been identified. The problem comes in trying to reconcile the physical evidence with Pliny and Josephus. The former described the Essene community on the west side of the Dead Sea as having renounced all sexual desire. Josephus's description of Essene practices begins by agreeing with Pliny that the Essenes shunned pleasure, passion, and marriage, but concludes with a long section that states that there was another order of Essenes which believed that complete rejection of marriage denied the chief function of life—the propagation of the race. They held, says Josephus, that if all people were to live celibate existences the whole race would quickly die out.[76]

If Josephus is correct that pockets of married Essenes did exist among the celibate, it becomes impossible to know without further excavation of the cemeteries just which group of Essenes lived at Qumran. Several proposals have been proffered. Perhaps the most reasonable scenario postulates that the Qumranites were an isolated male society—a celibate subsect of Essenes (either temporarily or permanently celibate we cannot tell)—who gave a proper burial to visiting relatives or travelers in the arid region who died suddenly. Of course, it is also possible to propose that both types of Essenes lived at Qumran by postulating that the community was not celibate at every stage of its history.[77]

One thing we *are* certain of is that the temple, ritual washings and cleanliness, the proper observance of feasts, festivals, and ordinances were at the absolute center of life at Qumran. The sectaries believed that the Jerusalem Temple's priesthood was thoroughly corrupt, and as a result, so was the calendar they perpetuated in the Holy City. Thus the covenanters refused to celebrate even such holy days as the Feast of Tabernacles and the Day of Atonement at the Jerusalem Temple, preferring instead to commemorate them in their own community without burnt offerings. Nevertheless, as the *Temple Scroll* indicates, the idea of a pure and undefiled temple in their midst remained their great ideal. One scholar has written that "the Essenes' basic ideal for living was to live as if they were priests dwelling in the temple itself. By this means, they sought to make their community a virtual temple, whether or not they were priests or Levites."[78] The Qumran covenanters often wore white linen garments to symbolize the level of templelike purity they sought to attain.[79]

One of the most fascinating and important aspects of life at Qumran was centered on a calendrical system different from the one used in the Jerusalem Temple from sometime in the second century B.C. until the great destruction in A.D. 70. For the sake of simplification, let us say that the system used by the Qumran covenanters combined solar, lunar, and ecclesiastical calendars. They observed a unique festival cycle in which they did not celebrate Jewish holidays and religious feasts on the same days such memorial services were celebrated by the rest of Judaism.

In addition, through divine revelation (as they believed), the Qumranites instituted and observed festivals not extant among other Israelites. The additional festivals included the Festival of New Wine, the Festival of New Oil, and the Wood Festival. The unique calendar of the Qumran community shows the distinctive and separatist outlook of that branch of Judaism.

Some of what we have noted concerning the beliefs and practices of the Essenes at Qumran may seem to describe either a pre-Christian era "gospel" community, or even a long-lost group of ancient Latter-day Saints with their familiar-sounding emphasis on consecration, templeworthy behavior, a strict probationary period before full membership was granted, priesthood organization, an expanded corpus of scripture, the apostate condition of the world, the term *Saints* being applied to covenant members, new ordinances and religious festivals, and light-darkness dualism. But such is not the case.

While the Qumran sectaries were a unified community that keenly recognized the apostate condition of Judaism and inaugurated reforms refocusing their own lives on the seminal tenets of true religion under the Mosaic dispensation, they also embraced notions contrary to the gospel of Jesus Christ. The Qumran community believed that the lame, halt, blind, deaf, and idiots remained in the care of the angels, and thus they did not admit them to their group. They did not believe that anyone had the right to worship in the name of the Lord unless a *minyan* (quorum) of ten individuals were gathered in the company of a priest. Contrast this with Jesus' statement that whenever two or more were gathered together in the name of the Lord, there his spirit would be also (compare Matthew 18:19–20).

Among the other differences between Qumran beliefs and the gospel of Christ that might be presented, a final one is worth noting here. As several scholars have pointed out, Jesus, in his Sermon on the Mount, flatly contradicts the idea that we should love our neighbors and hate our enemies:

> Ye have heard that it hath been said, Thou shalt love thy neighbor and hate thine enemy. But I say unto you, Love your enemies, bless them that curse you, do good to them that hate you, and pray for them which despitefully use you, and persecute you. (Matthew 5:43–44)

However, hating one's spiritual enemies is precisely what the *Rule of the Community* advocates in two separate sections: "Love all that He [God] has chosen and hate all that He has rejected"; also, "These are the rules of conduct for the Master in those times with respect to his loving and hating. Everlasting hatred in a spirit of secrecy for the men of perdition!"[80] Thus it seems clear that some points of Jesus' doctrine were an intentional rebuttal of Essene teaching.

## The Documents of the Community

Unlike their rabbinic contemporaries, the people of Qumran did not immediately (if ever) develop the notion of a closed canon. They obviously invested some of their own writings—the indigenous or sectarian texts—with the same (perhaps even greater?) authority and holiness as held by the Bible. These foundation documents of the Qumran covenanters reveal an attachment to and profound belief in the continuity of biblical Israel, prophesy, and covenental renewal. Based on a list compiled by Professor Talmon,[81] these foundation documents (the majority of which come from Cave 1) may be summarized as follows:

The *Damascus Document* (CD), sometimes called the *Zadokite Rule,* includes a compressed survey of the history of the *yaḥad,* along with a selection of legal materials, written in a style somewhat reminiscent of the biblical book of Deuteronomy. The historical account and the statutes appear to pertain to the entire "Community of the Renewed Covenant," that is, to the members who live with their families in "camps" in various locations in Palestine, as well as to the relatively small commune of members (all male?) who resided at Qumran, perhaps for only a season.

The *Rule of the Community* (1QS), or *Manual of Discipline* as it is often called, lists the precepts, structure, and public procedures of the community, and prescribes the conduct of its members.

The *Messianic Rule* (1QSa) offers a description of an envisioned messianic banquet based on the kind of common meals engaged in by the covenanters at Qumran. It also describes a future general assembly for the members of the community, at which time all precepts of the covenant will be publicly read before the entire community—priests, Levites and lay-Israelites, men and women alike, and also children who are mature enough to understand the proceedings (1QSa I 1–5). Professor Talmon asserts that this gathering is, in fact, a replica of Nehemiah's "great convocation" (see Nehemiah 8).[82]

The *War Rule* (1QM) presents legal and descriptive details of the cataclysmic war in which the Sons of Light (the Qumran covenanters) will finally overcome all Sons of Darkness (the wicked). In the ensuing era of universal peace, the covenanters will reestablish the temple in the New Jerusalem, the capital of their messianic kingdom, which is "a glorified reflection of Israel's historical commonwealth."[83]

The *Temple Scroll* (11QTemple) describes a future purified temple to be established as the ritual center for Israel. This document somewhat resembles the books of the Law, but it is God, not Moses, who directly addresses the people in the *Temple Scroll.*

The *Pesher Habakkuk* (1QpHab) or *Habakkuk Commentary,* as well as portions of other *pesharim* (commentaries), provide information on some aspects of the covenanters' history by interpreting certain nonhistorical texts of the Hebrew Bible as referring to historical events and historical people. In other words, the authors of these pesharim interpret the scriptural texts as foreshadowings of the historical experiences of their community. The Kittim, for example, in the commentaries on Habakkuk and Nahum are represented as instruments of God, appointed to punish the ungodly priests in Jerusalem. It is believed that the Kittim were the Romans.

*Miqsat Ma'aseh ha-Torah* (4QMMT) is a pieced-together collection of the fragments of copies of a document from Cave 4 that provides supplementary information on the outlook and function of the community.

These foundation documents are addressed specifically to the people of the Qumran community. The legal prescriptions contained in them are not considered debatable: "Based on inspiration, they are binding ... [and] are 'handed down' like biblical ordinances."[84] Thus the scrolls used by the people of Qumran have provided valuable information about a complex time period to which Latter-day Saints (and all Christians for that matter) trace their own spiritual roots. Is there any value for Latter-day Saints in studying the Dead Sea Scrolls? As we compare and contrast some of our own ideas and practices with those at Qumran, perhaps we can better appreciate the ancient people of that covenant community, and better understand the significant rifts in Christian-era Judaism. We can also appreciate the interconnectedness of ideas and texts across dispensations. The Dead Sea Scrolls have also given to the world the oldest biblical manuscripts and they help us to understand the history of our modern version of the Bible. And while caution needs to be urged in making more of the parallels between the Qumran sect and Mormonism than is appropriate, we can certainly see how some of the theological ideas found in the Church of Jesus Christ of Latter-day Saints are perfectly at home in an authentic ancient cultural milieu.

## Summary and Conclusions

We end where we began. Truly the most fascinating thing about the scrolls is the people who used them. Without the realization that the scrolls were the product of real people in a definite point in time, reflecting their fears, hopes, convictions, expectations, aims, and desires, the scrolls would be much less meaningful. By looking closely at the ancient people of Qumran—what they thought and how they behaved—we are given an extraordinary window of insight into the religious climate that spawned normative, or Pharisaic, Judaism, as well as another covenant group of dissenters—the early Christian contemporaries of the Qumran community. The people of Qumran stood at a historical juncture, a three-way crossroads in a period that witnessed the eventual survival of only two ideologies, Pharisaic, or rabbinic, Judaism and Christianity.

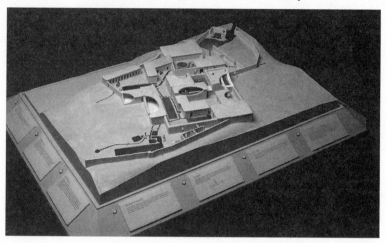

Model of Qumran based on excavations of the ruins. The map on page 119 can help you identify the various areas of the Qumran settlement. (Model by Michael Lyon, photograph by David Hawkinson.)

## Notes

1. See Frank Moore Cross, *The Ancient Library of Qumran*, 3rd ed. (Minneapolis: Fortress Press, 1995), 55–6.

2. See Eusebius, *The History of the Church from Christ to Constantine*, trans. G. A. Williamson (London: Penguin Books, 1989), 6:16. See also Charles F. Pfeiffer, *The Dead Sea Scrolls and the Bible* (New York: Weathervane Books, 1969), 11–2.

3. James C. VanderKam, *The Dead Sea Scrolls Today* (Grand Rapids, Mich.: Eerdmans, 1994), 1–2, quotes the pertinent portion of the letter.

4. See Pfeiffer, *Dead Sea Scrolls and the Bible*, 13.

5. The story of the find and its initial announcement can be found in most introductions to the Dead Sea Scrolls, but the most accurate without being pedantic is perhaps VanderKam, *Dead Sea Scrolls Today*, 3–8.

6. As cited in VanderKam, *Dead Sea Scrolls Today*, pl. 2.

7. See Hershel Shanks, "Barview," *Biblical Archaeology Review* 11/5 (1985): 4.

8. See Cross, *Ancient Library of Qumran*, 36–7.

9. See Joseph A. Fitzmyer, *Responses to 101 Questions on the Dead Sea Scrolls* (New York: Paulist Press, 1992), 57.

10. See Jerome Murphy-O'Connor, *The Holy Land: An Archaeological Guide from Earliest Times to 1700*, 3rd ed. (New York: Oxford University Press, 1992), 395.

11. See ibid.

12. Alan D. Crown and Lena Cansdale, "Qumran: Was It an Essene Settlement?" *Biblical Archaeology Review* 20/5 (1994): 25–35, 73–4, 76–8. As early as 1959, Henry Del Medico argued that the structure in question was a triclinium rather than a Scriptorium. This interpretation was also favored by the great biblical scholar G. R. Driver.

13. Personal conversation with Dr. Broshi at the International Conference on the Dead Sea Scrolls, 15–17 July 1996, held at Brigham Young University, Provo, Utah.

14. Shemaryahu Talmon, *The "Dead Sea Scrolls" or "The Community of the Renewed Covenant"* (Tucson: University of Arizona Press, 1993), 6.

15. See VanderKam, *Dead Sea Scrolls Today*, 12.

16. See Fitzmyer, *Responses to 101 Questions*, 13.

17. See ibid., 26

18. See Pfeiffer, *Dead Sea Scrolls and the Bible*, 18.

19. Fitzmyer, *Responses to 101 Questions*, 26.

20. See Murphy-O'Connor, *The Holy Land*, 397.

21. Talmon, *"Dead Sea Scrolls,"* 3.

22. As cited in Yigael Yadin, *The Temple Scroll: The Hidden Law of the Dead Sea Sect* (London: Weidenfeld and Nicolson, 1985), 113.

23. Marion G. Romney, "Temples—The Gates to Heaven," *Ensign* (March 1971): 16.

24. See David B. Galbraith, D. Kelly Ogden, and Andrew C. Skinner, *Jerusalem: The Eternal City* (Salt Lake City: Deseret Book, 1996), 150.

25. See VanderKam, *Dead Sea Scrolls Today,* 71.

26. See Cross, *Ancient Library of Qumran,* 54.

27. Frank Moore Cross, "The Historical Context of the Scrolls," in *Understanding the Dead Sea Scrolls,* ed. Hershel Shanks (New York: Random House, 1992), 25.

28. Cross, "Historical Context," 25.

29. *Rule of the Community* (1QS) I and V. This and subsequent translations, unless otherwise noted, are from Geza Vermes, *The Dead Sea Scrolls in English,* 4th ed. (London: Penguin Books, 1995).

30. See the critique in VanderKam, *Dead Sea Scrolls Today,* 93–4.

31. For an introduction to the *Damascus Document,* sometimes called the *Zadokite Document,* see Geza Vermes, *The Dead Sea Scrolls: Qumran in Perspective* (Philadelphia: Fortress Press, 1981), 48–51.

32. *Damascus Document* (CD) I.

33. See VanderKam, *Dead Sea Scrolls Today,* 100–1.

34. See *Damascus Document* (CD) I; *Commentary on Psalm 37:7,* in *The Dead Sea Scriptures,* trans. Theodor H. Gaster, 3rd ed., (Garden City, N.Y.: Anchor Books, 1976), 326.

35. See VanderKam, *Dead Sea Scrolls Today,* 102.

36. See the summary in Hershel Shanks, "Essene Origins— Palestine or Babylonia," in *Understanding the Dead Sea Scrolls,* ed. Shanks, 80.

37. Cross, "Historical Context," 31.

38. Ibid., 31–2.

39. Pliny, *Natural History,* vol. 2, trans. H. Rackham, Loeb Classical Library (1969), 5.73.

40. These include Pliny's inference that the settlement was still in existence around the time he wrote in A.D. 77 because he used the present tense in his description. This present-tense language seems to contradict the generally accepted picture provided by archaeological data that suggest that the settlement was destroyed by the Romans in A.D. 68 or 70. The author's reference to Engedi as a city second only to Jerusalem in palm trees and fertility has also been criticized (it should probably read "Jeri-

cho") as indicative of the overall problematic nature of Pliny's description.

41. See VanderKam, *Dead Sea Scrolls Today*, 72.

42. As cited in ibid., 74.

43. See ibid., 87.

44. See ibid., 88–91.

45. Josephus, *Jewish War*, trans. H. Thackeray and R. Marcus, Loeb Classical Library (1988), 2.122.

46. *Rule of the Community* (1QS) VI.

47. Josephus, *Antiquities*, trans. H. Thackeray, Loeb Classical Library (1976), 13.171–3.

48. *Rule of the Community* (1QS) III.

49. Scroll terminology is not complicated, just abbreviated. The number 4 designates the cave in which the document was found (Cave 4 in this case), the Q stands for Qumran, and the last number indicates this text is fragment number 180.

50. *Ages of the Creation* (4Q180).

51. See the discussion in VanderKam, *Dead Sea Scrolls Today*, 153.

52. *Jubilees* 23:30–1, in *The Book of Jubilees*, trans. James VanderKam (Lovanii: E. Peeters, 1989), 511:149.

53. Josephus, *Jewish War* 2.154–5.

54. As cited in VanderKam, *Dead Sea Scrolls Today*, 81. The preliminary publication of this text is found in Emile Puech, *Revue de Qumran* 15 (1991–92): 479–522.

55. *Rule of the Community* (1QS) VI.

56. Ibid., V.

57. Ibid., VI.

58. Josephus, *Jewish War* 2.129–31.

59. Ibid., 2.123.

60. See the discussion in VanderKam, *Dead Sea Scrolls Today*, 81.

61. See ibid., 86.

62. Josephus, *Jewish War* 2.147–9.

63. *War Rule* (1QM) VII.

64. As cited in Yigael Yadin, *The Temple Scroll*, 178.

65. As cited in S. Kent Brown, "The Dead Sea Scrolls: A Mor-

mon Perspective," *BYU Studies* 23/1 (1983): 55.

66. *Rule of the Community* (1QS) VII.

67. Josephus, *Jewish War* 2.147.

68. As cited in Fitzmyer, *Responses to 101 Questions*, 53 (see pp. 53–6).

69. *Damascus Document* (CD) XIV. The use of brackets in the text indicates restored portions by the translator.

70. *War Rule* (1QM) II.

71. See Talmon, *"Dead Sea Scrolls,"* 15.

72. See ibid., 16.

73. *Rule of the Community* (1QS) VIII, in *Dead Sea Scriptures*; see also Vermes's translation.

74. These quotations are from the Mishnah, *Sotah* 48b, *Sanhedrin* 11a, and from Seder ʾOlam Rabbah 6, as cited in Talmon, *"Dead Sea Scrolls,"* 16.

75. Talmon, *"Dead Sea Scrolls,"* 17–8.

76. See Josephus, *Jewish War* 2.160–1.

77. See VanderKam, *Dead Sea Scrolls Today*, 14–5, 90–1.

78. Brown, "Dead Sea Scrolls: A Mormon Perspective," 57–8.

79. See Josephus, *Jewish War* 2.126–32.

80. *Rule of the Community* (1QS) I and IX.

81. See Talmon, *"Dead Sea Scrolls,"* 3–4.

82. See ibid., 3.

83. Ibid.

84. Ibid., 24

# CHAPTER 2

# THE CONTRIBUTION OF THE DEAD SEA SCROLLS TO BIBLICAL UNDERSTANDING

*Donald W. Parry*

Before the discovery of the Dead Sea Scrolls (DSS) in 1947, scholars used medieval manuscripts for much of their understanding of the Old Testament (Hebrew Bible). Two such manuscripts are the Cairo Codex of the Prophets, which dates to A.D. 895, and the Aleppo Codex, which dates to A.D. 925.[1] The biblical scrolls and fragments of the DSS, however, comprise texts that are one thousand years older than the previously known texts of the Hebrew Bible. Most of the biblical texts of the DSS date from 150 B.C. to A.D. 68,[2] although fragments from Exodus, Samuel, and Jeremiah have been dated to the middle of the third century B.C.[3]

With the scrolls in hand, we have learned much about the history, transmission, and appearance of the Old Testament texts during the last centuries of the Second Temple Period. We have gained a great deal of knowledge concerning ancient scribal practices, including paragraphing,

*Donald W. Parry is assistant professor of Hebrew language and literature at Brigham Young University.*

scribal corrections, and various other marks and notes in the text.[4] We have gained greater appreciation for the archaic practices of orthography (spelling practices), morphology (form of words), and epigraphy (inscriptions). Our knowledge of the development of Hebrew, Aramaic, and Greek languages and scripts has increased considerably. Perhaps most significantly, the discovery of the DSS biblical texts enables us to reconstruct portions of the Old Testament.

In this chapter I first make some preliminary remarks concerning the biblical texts discovered in the desert of Judea. Next I discuss a small sampling of the variant readings in the ancient biblical texts in light of the DSS and then demonstrate how the DSS have influenced many of the modern English translations of the Old Testament. I will refer to three major ancient versions of the Old Testament—the biblical texts of the DSS, the Hebrew Bible (called the Masoretic Text, or MT), and the Old Greek Bible (called the Septuagint, or LXX).

## Old Testament Texts at Qumran

Of the more than eight hundred scrolls and fragmented texts of the DSS discovered in caves near the Dead Sea region, approximately two hundred represent books from the Old Testament, such as Genesis, Isaiah, and Jeremiah.[5] The biblical scrolls' state of preservation varies considerably.[6] The great *Isaiah Scroll* of Cave 1 (1QIsaᵃ) comprises all sixty-six chapters of Isaiah, is twenty-four feet long, and averages ten inches in height. Similarly, the *Psalms Scroll* from Cave 11 is in a fair state of preservation. For the most part, however, the biblical books that have survived two millennia in the caves are extremely fragmented; many are no larger than the size of a postcard, and some fragments are as small as a postage stamp. Even the smallest fragment, however, can add to our knowledge of the Bible.

Qumran Cave 1, in which the first scrolls were discovered in 1947. The smaller upper opening is the original entrance, and the larger openings were made later by excavators. The great *Isaiah Scroll* and other significant community documents were discovered here. (Photograph courtesy Dana M. Pike.)

Biblical texts were discovered in many of the eleven so-called Qumran caves. For example, two Isaiah scrolls were discovered in Cave 1; three biblical fragments (Ezekiel 16:31–3; Psalms 2:6–7; Lamentations 1:10–2; 3:53–62) were found in Cave 3; a large number of biblical manuscripts were uncovered in Cave 4 (approximately fifteen thousand fragments of both biblical and sectarian documents); and Cave 11 produced two fragments of Leviticus (including one written in an old Hebrew script), one fragment of Deuteronomy, one fragment of Ezekiel, and four fragments of Psalms. In all, the distribution of biblical texts in the eleven caves of Qumran may be shown as follows:[7]

| Cave 1 | 17 texts | Cave 7 | 1 text |
|--------|----------|--------|--------|
| Cave 2 | 18 texts | Cave 8 | 2 texts |
| Cave 3 | 3 texts | Cave 9 | 0 texts |
| Cave 4 | 137 texts | Cave 10 | 0 texts |
| Cave 5 | 7 texts | Cave 11 | 10 texts |
| Cave 6 | 7 texts | | |

Discoveries of nineteen other Biblical texts were also made at Masada, Wadi Murabbaʾat, and Nahal Hever, all of which are located in the Judean desert.

With the exception of the book of Esther, every book of the Old Testament has been found in the Qumran caves. That the book of Esther was not among the other biblical books should not trouble us: "While several explanations are possible for the absence of Esther, the most likely is simple chance. A finding of zero copies is neither surprising nor statistically meaningful, for several other books of the Writings are found in only one or two copies."[8] Multiple copies of books (although most are extremely fragmented) have been located. The following table lists the number of biblical manuscripts discovered among the DSS:[9]

| Genesis | 15 | Twelve Prophets | 8 |
|---------|-----|-----------------|-----|
| Exodus | 17 | Psalms | 36 |
| Leviticus | 13 | Proverbs | 2 |
| Numbers | 8 | Job | 4 |
| Deuteronomy | 29 | Song of Solomon | 4 |
| Joshua | 2 | Ruth | 4 |
| Judges | 3 | Lamentations | 4 |
| 1–2 Samuel | 4 | Ecclesiastes | 3 |
| 1–2 Kings | 3 | Esther | 0 |
| Isaiah | 21 | Daniel | 8 |
| Jeremiah | 6 | Ezra–Nehemiah | 1 |
| Ezekiel | 6 | 1–2 Chronicles | 1 |

VanderKam notes that "the raw totals [of the biblical books discovered among the Dead Sea Scrolls] probably also indicate which books were used frequently";[10] that is, Psalms (36 copies), Deuteronomy (29 copies), and Isaiah (21

This page of column 34 of the *Isaiah Scroll* begins in the upper right-hand corner and should be read from right to left. It shows the use of paragraphs two thousand years ago. Marks like the three on the left-hand column (two are x's and the other looks like a cowboy hat) are found throughout the text, but we do not know what they mean. On the fourth line from the bottom, between two lines, is an added word. A dot on each side indicates where the word was inserted to correct the mistake. (Photography by John C. Trever.)

copies) were likely held in great esteem by the inhabitants of Qumran.[11] The historical books (e.g., Joshua, Judges, 1–2 Samuel, 1–2 Kings, and Chronicles) were probably less important to the religious goals of the Qumranites.

Most of the biblical scrolls are written in Hebrew,[12] the language of the ancient Israelites and the sacred language of the Jews. A few manuscripts including the book of Daniel, the apocryphal book of Tobit, a fragment of a *targum* (translation) of the book of Job, and fragments of the book of Enoch are written in Aramaic (a language that resembles and is closely related to Hebrew), the language adopted by the Jews after seventy years of exile in Babylon. In addition, a number of Old Testament manuscripts are preserved in Greek.

The majority of texts are copied on animal skin, although a few papyrus texts do exist. Black ink is consistently used, with the exception of certain verses of the book of Numbers (4QNum[b]) that are written in red ink (Numbers 20:22–3; 22:21; 23:13, 27; 31:25, 28, 48; 32:25; 33:1).

New Testament texts, of course, were not discovered among the DSS. The reason for this is twofold: first and foremost, the sect who inhabited the community were *not* Christians; and second, the texts belonging to the corpus of the DSS were created and copied before the rise of Christianity in the first century A.D.

## *Tefillin* **and** *Mezuzot*

Other biblical texts, in the form of small parchments containing passages from Exodus and Deuteronomy, have been excavated at Qumran. The parchments were part of *tefillin* (called phylacteries in the New Testament; see Matthew 23:5) and *mezuzot* (small boxes fastened to the door posts of some Jewish houses or structures). The texts are usually from Exodus 12:43–13:16 and Deuteronomy 5:1–6:9, 10:12–11:21. Twenty-one tefillin texts and eight mezuzot texts have been found in the Qumran excavations.

## Old Testament Pseudepigrapha, Apocrypha, and Commentaries

In addition to the various books of the Old Testament listed above, the DSS include a number of commentaries on individual books of the Old Testament[13]—including Isaiah, Habakkuk, Hosea, Micah, Nahum, and the Psalms—that reveal a striking method of biblical interpretation. In these commentaries, the passage of scripture is first quoted, followed by an interpretation. The author(s) of the commentary frequently liken the passage to the Qumran community of believers by arguing that its fulfillment had reference either to themselves or to contemporary events.

For example, a passage in the *Commentary on the Psalms* quotes Psalm 37:10: "A little while and the wicked shall be no more; I will look towards his place but he shall not be there." The interpretation follows: "At the end of forty years {from the time that the commentary was written} the wicked will perish and not an [evil] man shall be found on the earth."[14] In a passage in the *Commentary on Habakkuk,* the interest in the last days can also be seen: "And God told Habakkuk to write down that which would happen to the final generation, but He did not make known to him when time would come to an end."[15]

Several Apocryphal[16] or Pseudepigraphic[17] texts were excavated in the caves, including writings that were previously known to the world—Tobit, Sirach, a Letter of Jeremiah (Baruch 6), Psalm 151, *Enoch (1 Enoch), Jubilees,* and the *Testaments of the Twelve Patriarchs.* Other writings of an apocryphal nature were unknown to the world at the time of their discovery and represent new texts. These texts possess the names of or are generally affiliated with well-known Old Testament characters such as Noah, Jacob, Joseph, Amran, Moses, Joshua, Samuel, David, Jeremiah, Ezekiel, Daniel, and Esther.[18] These texts offer scholars a treasure chest of information into the socioreligious world of Second Temple Jews and their language, rituals, worship, etc.

## Variant Readings and Errors in the Text of the Bible

Although the DSS biblical texts bring us one thousand years closer to the original words of the prophets, we still do not have the so-called autograph texts, that is, those which were penned by the prophets (or the scribes of the prophets) themselves. We possess copies of the apograph texts, which were created several hundred years after the autograph texts. Throughout the history of the various biblical texts, both the Old and the New Testaments, various errors have crept in—a fact that scholars have been aware of for centuries. The Jewish Talmud, which dates to the fifth century A.D., lists eighteen occasions when the scribes intentionally altered the Old Testament because they thought certain ideas showed disrespect for God, or because certain ideas disagreed with the scribes' theological notion of who or what God is. These textual changes, called *tiqqune sopherim* (errors of the scribes) may be found in the following verses: Genesis 18:22; Numbers 11:15; 12:12; 1 Samuel 3:13; 2 Samuel 16:12; 20:1; 1 Kings 12:16; Jeremiah 2:11; Ezekiel 8:17; Hosea 4:7; Habakkuk 1:12; Zechariah 2:12; Malachi 1:13; Psalm 106:20; Job 7:20; 32:3; 2 Chronicles 10:16; and Lamentations 3:20.[19]

In this same light, James C. VanderKam notes that the

Samaritan Pentateuch (the Samaritan version of the five books of Moses) "differs from the Masoretic Text in some six thousand readings; most of these are minor matters such as different spellings of words."[20] A few variant readings in the Samaritan Pentateuch are not minor; rather, they represent intentional theological changes dealing with the temple and temple worship. Emanuel Tov presents evidence of such theological changes:

> The main ideological change in [the Samaritan Pentateuch] concerns the central place of worship. In every verse in the Hebrew Bible in which Jerusalem is alluded to as the central place of worship, the Samaritans have inserted in its stead, sometimes by way of allusion, their own center, Mount Gerizim.[21]

The Samaritans believed that Mount Gerizim represented the temple of Israel, not the temple built by Solomon in Jerusalem. This Samaritan approach to the temple and temple worship becomes apparent in an examination of the Decalogue (Ten Commandments). Here the Samaritan Pentateuch alters the Decalogue so that the first of the Ten Commandments serves as a mere introduction, and adds a tenth commandment that refers "to the sanctity of Mount Gerizim."[22]

Variant readings are frequent in the ancient versions and textual witnesses of the Old Testament. Students of biblical Hebrew simply need to look at the footnotes (called the critical apparatus) of the scholars' edition of the Hebrew Bible (entitled *Biblia Hebraica Stuttgartensia*) to discover that variant readings are listed on every page of the Bible.

The New Testament, like the Old, was contaminated through long centuries of transmission. "There are over 5,200 Greek New Testament manuscripts, no two of which are alike. They come from different areas and communities in antiquity and that accounts for some differences."[23]

Bart D. Ehrman points out in his *The Orthodox Corruption of Scripture* that John Mill's critical apparatus of the Greek New Testament makes reference to approximately 100 Greek manuscripts and shows "some 30,000 variant readings."[24] As Ehrman demonstrates, many of the variant readings are intentional theological changes.

Even after the printing press was invented, errors still occurred in different printings of the Bible. The first edition of the King James Version (KJV), printed in 1611, contained a number of errors, some of which were corrected in the 1612 edition, followed by an additional 413 corrections and changes made in the 1613 edition. For instance, the 1611 edition read, "then cometh Judas" instead of "then cometh Jesus" (Matthew 26:36); "strain out a gnat" rather than the correct "strain at a gnat" (Matthew 23:24); and "approved to death" in place of "appointed to death" (1 Corinthians 4:9).[25] As early as 1659, one scholar noted that some "20,000 errors . . . had crept into the six different editions printed in the 1650s."[26]

Other editions have been named after major errors that have crept into the text. The so-called "Wicked Bible" was so named because the word *not* was omitted in the seventh commandment; the "Unrighteous Bible" was entitled such because it stated that the *unrighteous* would inherit the kingdom of God; and the "Vinegar Bible" set forth the "Parable of the Vinegar." Though a few of these changes deal with major historical or theological issues, most are fairly insignificant and deal with spelling changes or minor variant readings.

Joseph Smith was fully aware that errors existed in the text of the Bible, as is witnessed by his inspired contribution to biblical studies that we call the *Joseph Smith Translation*, by the Book of Mormon texts that parallel biblical passages (especially Isaiah), and by statements he made during his sermons. On one occasion the Prophet taught, "I believe the Bible as it read when it came from the pen of the original writers." He then detailed reasons why errors exist in the scriptures: "Ignorant translators, careless transcribers, or designing and corrupt priests have committed many errors."[27]

## Causes of Textual Corruptions

Texual critics categorize the three major types of textual changes or variant readings in the Bible as pluses, minuses, and changes.[28] We define a plus as "a portion of a text not found in another text"; a minus as "a portion of text that is missing in comparison to another text";[29] and changes as differences that neither shorten nor lengthen the text but that present variant readings. Most variant readings were unintentional or accidental but some were intentional or deliberate, produced by scribes who desired to explain portions of the text or alter the texts according to their theological concerns. William Hugh Brownlee has summarized the causes of variant readings:

> There are numerous examples of the interchange of letters which are similar in appearance or in sound: the former are errors of the eye; the latter, errors of the ear. These errors in a manuscript might be cumulative from a series of copyists. On the other hand, both kinds of error might occur all in the same process. Thus a scribe in copying a manuscript directly by himself might misread certain words because of their similar appearance. If he read as much as a whole sentence to himself before transcribing it, it would be possible for him to make a few mistakes of "hearing," due to his habit of thinking orally rather than visually. Similarly, if a manuscript were being read aloud by a reader in a scriptorium, with scribes gathered about a table, each of them copying by the ear,

errors of seeing and of hearing could both be made. The reader might sometimes misread; and the scribes might not always understand the words, especially if the reader did not enunciate clearly. . . .

There were also mechanical errors of inverting the order of letters (metathesis); of copying letters or words twice (errors of dittography); of transcribing letters or words only once which should occur twice (haplography); of omitting one of two phrases which began similarly (homoioarchton) or ended similarly (homoioteleuton), the eye accidentally skipping from the first occurrence of the initial or final word to its second occurrence.[30]

"Errors of the ear" are common in the text and may arise when the text is dictated to a scribe, or when the text is heard and not seen. An example of such an error is the expression *you can see four miles,* which may be heard as *you can see for miles.* A common Hebrew error that falls in this category is the particle *lo* (לו) or *lo* (לא), two homonyms that are translated as "to him" or "no, not."

"Errors of the eye" may be the result of a scribe attempting to read the handwriting of an earlier scribe, whose bookhand is often illegible or who used an archaic script. Such errors include the confusion of letters that look similar. In the English, such letters include *m* and *n, b* and *d, o* and *c, u* and *v, v* and *w,* or *v* and *y.* Similar looking letters in the Hebrew alphabet include ד and ר, ה and ח, ו and י, or ח and ת. Another scribal error results from the incorrect division of letters and words. For example, the letters *Godisnowhere,* designed to be read "God is now here," may be misread as "God is nowhere."

Many errors originate from the copyist's carelessness or human fallibility. A scribe may be tired, incompetent, physically or emotionally ill, or his eyes may inadvertently skip or duplicate a single word or an entire line of text.

## Examples of Errors

A striking example of a lost passage of scripture has been discovered in the DSS texts of Samuel. The new passage, which belongs in 1 Samuel 11:1,[31] presents some forty-nine Hebrew words that are missing in the Hebrew Bible as well as the other ancient textual witnesses.[32] With the restoration of this passage, there is a better transition from the final verse in chapter 10 to the first verse in chapter 11, and the context for the story of King Nahash is now in place:

> And Nahash, king of the children of Ammon, oppressed harshly the Gadites and the Reubenites. He would gouge out the right eye of each of them and would not grant Israel a deliverer. No one was left of the Israelites across the Jordan whose right eye Nahash, king of the Ammonites, had not gouged out. But there were seven thousand men who had fled from the Ammonites and had entered Jabesh-gilead. (1 Samuel 11:1)[33]

The paragraph helps students of the Bible understand the situation described in chapter 11 concerning the advancement of Nahash and his troops against Jabesh-gilead and the Israelites. It was the plan of Nahash to make a treaty with the Israelites who were dwelling in Jabesh-gilead, on the condition that he "gouge out the right eye of each person in the city," rendering them helpless in rebelling against him. The Israelites, however, rally around King Saul and the prophet Samuel (11:5–7), slay a number of Ammonites, and cause the remainder to flee. Samuel and Saul give credit to the Lord for their victory.

Many other missing texts have been discovered among the DSS, many of which may be writings inspired of God. These include Psalm 151, which is included in the Septuagint but missing in the Hebrew Bible. The Psalm deals with King David, his call from the Lord, and his defeat of Goliath. Previously unknown psalms found at Qumran include the "Prayer for Deliverance," "Apostrophe to Zion," and "Hymn to the Creator." Newly discovered prosaic texts include "David's Compositions," the "Prayer of Nabonidus," and a letter of Jeremiah.

Chapter 1 of the DSS Samuel texts (4QSam^a)[34] features a number of variant readings. I will list six examples:

1 Samuel 1:11

> and no razor shall *pass over* his head (DSS Samuel)
>> shall *go up on* his head (MT, LXX)

1 Samuel 1:13

> And *Hannah*, she spoke in her heart
> (The name Hannah is lacking in the DSS Samuel, but is found in MT, LXX)

1 Samuel 1:18

> Then the woman went to her quarters, and ate *and drank with her husband*
> (italics represent a plus found in the DSS Samuel)

1 Samuel 1:22

> [Hannah] said to her husband, As soon as the child is weaned, I will bring him, that he may appear in the presence of the LORD, and remain there forever; *I will offer him as a nazarite all the days of his life*
> (italics represent an addition found in the DSS Samuel)

1 Samuel 1:23

> Elkanah said to her, Do what seems best to you, wait until you have weaned him, only, may the LORD establish *that which goes out of your mouth* (DSS Samuel, LXX)
> *his word* (MT)

1 Samuel 1:24

> When she had weaned him, she took him up with her, along with *three bulls* (MT)
> along with *a three year old bull* (DSS Samuel, LXX)

There is not sufficient room in this paper to discuss the import of these variant readings. They are set forth for the purpose of demonstrating the types of variations that exist in ancient copies of the Bible.

## Theological Changes

Scholars have produced evidence that textual changes were made based on a specific theological stance or agenda held by scribes or others who have had control of various biblical texts at one point or another in history. P. Kyle McCarter's *Textual Criticism: Recovering the Text of the Hebrew Bible* discusses a number of theological changes, including euphemistic insertions, euphemistic substitutions, harmonizing substitutions, and suppressed readings.[35] For a thorough examination of theological variant readings in the New Testament, see Ehrman's *The Orthodox Corruption of Scripture*, cited above. Emanuel Tov's *Textual Criticism of the Hebrew Bible* lists several examples of variant readings that relate to God's appearance to humans:[36]

"I shall never see the Lord" (Isaiah 38:11) (MT)
"I shall never see the salvation of God" (LXX)

"the Lord met him" (Exodus 4:24) (MT)
"the angel of the Lord met him" (LXX)

"and Moses went up to God" (Exodus 19:3) (MT)
"and Moses went up to the mountain of God" (LXX)

"and they saw the God of Israel" (Exodus 24:10) (MT)
"and they saw the place where the God of Israel stood" (LXX)

"and he beholds the likeness of the LORD" (Num. 12:8) (MT)
"and he beholds the glory of the LORD" (LXX)

In every instance above, the LXX presents a different picture than the MT. The words of the MT indicate that humans can access and even see God, while the text of the LXX never directly states the notion that humans are able to behold God. Tov points out "anti-polytheistic alterations"[37] that have taken place at some point in the transmission of the Bible. Although the examples given above are not drawn from the DSS library, they illustrate the types of variations that may be found in the ancient textual witnesses.

## The Case of the Divine Name in the DSS Samuel Texts

One can see certain tendencies in sections of the Hebrew Bible that favor the sacred epithet *God* (Hebrew, *Elohim*) over the divine name *LORD* (Hebrew, *Jehovah* or *YHWH*, called the Tetragrammaton),[38] presumably for theological reasons. An examination of the book of Chronicles reveals that the chronicler preferred the term *Elohim* "even where his sources (e.g., Samuel and Kings) had employed the divine name YHWH."[39] One large section of the Psalms (chapters 42–83), shows a marked preference for the divine name *Elohim* rather than *Jehovah*, whereas the remaining Psalms frequently use the Tetragrammaton throughout. It has been suggested on more than one occasion that a scribe who was perhaps connected with the Jerusalem Temple reworked Psalms 42–83, and for pious reasons frequently substituted *Elohim* for *Jehovah*.[40]

The poetic sections of Job lack the Tetragrammaton in favor of other divine names, with two notable exceptions (12:9; 28:28).[41] *Jehovah* is not attested in the book of Daniel (with the exception of the prayer of Daniel in chapter 9); both the books of Daniel and Ecclesiastes prefer the epithet *Elohim*.[42] The preference for the name *Elohim* is also found in the memoirs of both Ezra (Ezra 7:27–10:17) and Nehemiah

(Nehemiah 1–6; 12:27–13:31); and here it is appropriate to mention that neither of the divine names *Jehovah* nor *Elohim* is used in the Song of Songs[43] or the book of Esther.[44]

The extent to which scribes contributed to the preference of the epithet *Elohim* over the name *Jehovah* in certain Hebrew texts is unclear; neither is it clear why the divine names *Jehovah* and *Elohim* are not found in the Song of Songs or Esther. Choices in favor of the name *Elohim* may have been made by the chronicler as well as by the redactor of the Psalms.

M. H. Segal summarizes the prevailing view of scholars concerning the avoidance of the Tetragrammaton and the preference of *Elohim* when he argues that during the post-exilic period, "a heightened sense of the sanctity of Deity and of the sacredness of its own proper name led to the avoidance of a too frequent employment of the name Yhwh (Jehovah) which gradually became ineffable, and to its replacement by a synonymous substitute. The first stage in this tendency was the revival of the use of Elohim which appears clearly in the book of Chronicles."[45]

In a previously published paper, I examined the seventeen occasions when one or more of the divine names

Professor Donald W. Parry studying fragments of *4QSamuel* in the Rockefeller Museum, Jerusalem.

*Jehovah* and *Elohim* appears as a variant reading in the Qumran text of Samuel (4QSam^a)[46] when compared with the Hebrew Bible and the Old Greek Bible.[47] I concluded in that paper that the DSS texts of Samuel prefer the name *Jehovah* in places where the Hebrew Bible prefers the name *Elohim*.[48] Of the seventeen variant readings, the Hebrew Bible avoids or lacks the Tetragrammaton on twelve occasions. If one discounts the three secondary pluses belonging to 4QSam^a (1 Samuel 1:22; 5:11; 11:9) when the name *Jehovah* appears to have been added, we are still left with nine occasions when the Hebrew Bible lacks the Tetragrammaton. There is one occasion when the Hebrew Bible reads *Jehovah* against 4QSam^a, which reads *Elohim* (2 Samuel 12:15).

## Using the DSS Biblical Texts in Modern English Translations

Contemporary translation committees of the Bible hold the DSS in high regard. On a number of occasions the committees have departed from traditional readings of 1 Samuel in favor of new readings. The New International Version has preferred the readings of the DSS texts of 1 Samuel on fifteen occasions over the readings of the traditional Hebrew text; the New American Bible has shown even more loyalty to the DSS by choosing 230 readings from the DSS (and LXX) over the traditional text. The other versions, as shown on the list below, have used variant readings from the DSS to varying degrees. The following list features six prominent English translations:[49]

| Translation | Use of Variant Readings |
|---|---|
| New International Version | 15 |
| Today's English Version | 51 |
| Revised Standard Version | about 60 |
| New Revised Standard Version | about 110 |

New English Bible                    160
New American Bible                   230

The New King James Version (NKJV) (1982), which is not listed above, does not share the same devotion to the DSS texts. Only on one occasion does it prefer a variant reading from the DSS book of 1 Samuel; in fact, it relies on the DSS on only six occasions in the entire Old Testament (Deuteronomy 32:43; 1 Samuel 1:24; Isaiah 10:16, 22:8, 38:14, 49:5).[50]

According to Harold Scanlin, a translation adviser for the United Bible Societies, "every major Bible translation published since 1950 has claimed to have taken into account the textual evidence of the DSS."[51] Many of these recent English translations have gone through subsequent revisions to incorporate the variant readings from the DSS. For instance, the Revised Standard Version (1952) is now the New Revised Standard Version (1990), the New English Bible (1970) was revised to the Revised English Bible (1989), the Jerusalem Bible (1966) is now the New Jerusalem Bible (1985), and the New American Bible (1970) is going through a major revision at the present time.

I do not want to give the impression that a great number of theological or historical variant readings of the DSS have great significance for the student of the Bible. The Bible went through a remarkable history to make it into this century, especially in view of the ancient methods of transmitting texts by hand, sometimes in primitive conditions, and considering that the scribes lacked photocopy machines, computers, printing presses, and similar modern inventions. Individuals should not lose faith in this wonderful wealth of prophetic material called the Old Testament, which contains baskets of precious jewels and barrels of pearls. A single page of the Old Testament (with the exception of the Song of Songs) is worth more than all of the gold and silver in the entire world. I personally treasure the writings of all of the prophets in the scriptures, and now have the added benefit of examining the new readings provided by the DSS.

# Notes

1. See James C. VanderKam, *The Dead Sea Scrolls Today* (Grand Rapids, Mich.: Eerdmans, 1994), 123.

2. Other texts of the Judean desert have different dates; that is, the texts from Nahal Hever, Wadi Murabba'at, and Masada date from about 250 B.C. to A.D. 135.

3. The dates of these three manuscripts are as follows: 4QSam$^b$, ca. 250 B.C.; 4QJer$^a$, ca. 200 B.C.; and 4QExod$^f$, ca. 275–225 B.C. See David Noel Freedman, "The Massoretic Text and the Qumran Scrolls: A Study in Orthography," *Textus* 2 (1962): 87–102; republished in *Qumran and the History of the Biblical Text*, ed. Frank Moore Cross and Shemaryahu Talmon (Cambridge: Harvard University Press, 1975), 196–211.

4. See Emanuel Tov, "Scribal Markings in the Texts from the Judean Desert," in *Current Research and Technological Developments: Proceedings of the Conference on the Judaean Desert Scrolls, Jerusalem, 30 April 1995*, ed. Donald W. Parry and Stephen D. Ricks (Leiden: E. J. Brill, 1996), 41–77.

5. For a listing of biblical passages discovered among the DSS, see Eugene Ulrich, "An Index of the Passages in the Biblical Manuscripts from the Judean Desert (Genesis–Kings)," *Dead Sea Discoveries* 1 (1994): 113–29; and Eugene Ulrich, "An Index of the Passages in the Biblical Manuscripts from the Judean Desert (Part 2: Isaiah–Chronicles)," *Dead Sea Discoveries* 2 (1995): 86–107.

6. See P. W. Skehan, "Qumran IV. Littérature de Qumran," *Supplément au Dictionnaire de la Bible* 9 (1978): 805–28, gives a physical description of the biblical fragments.

7. See VanderKam, *Dead Sea Scrolls Today*, 31.

8. Lawrence H. Schiffman, *Reclaiming the Dead Sea Scrolls* (Philadelphia: Jewish Publication Society, 1994), 164.

9. See VanderKam, *The Dead Sea Scrolls Today*, 30. It should be noted that VanderKam's list is preliminary; in due time scholars will be able to list, with some definiteness, how many biblical texts were discovered at Qumran. For a slightly different list of extant DSS biblical texts compare Schiffman, *Reclaiming the Dead Sea Scrolls*, 163.

10. VanderKam, *Dead Sea Scrolls Today*, 31.

11. It is probably more than coincidence that the early Christian community held the same three Old Testament writings—Psalms, Deuteronomy, and Isaiah—to be of great value, for they are the most quoted scriptural books in the New Testament.

12. The majority of the Hebrew manuscripts were written in square Hebrew characters, known as Assyrian script or Aramaic script, although several texts were copied in paleo-Hebrew script.

13. See VanderKam, *Dead Sea Scrolls Today*, 152–3.

14. *Commentary on Psalms* (4Q171) II, in Geza Vermes, *The Dead Sea Scrolls in English*, 4th ed. (New York: Penguin Books, 1995).

15. *Commentary on Habakkuk* (1QpHab) VII, in ibid.

16. In this paper the word *Apocrypha* is a cover term used for the books that are included in the Catholic version of the Old Testament (derived from the Old Greek translation, or Septuagint) but not included in most Protestant Old Testaments. Apocryphal books include Tobit, Judith, 1–2 Maccabees, Wisdom, Sirach, Baruch, and additional sections in Esther and Daniel.

17. *Pseudepigrapha* is a term used by scholars to represent several Jewish religious books written or extant between the fourth century B.C. and second century A.D. that did not become part of the Hebrew Bible: "One could characterize [pseudepigrapha] as a reverse form of plagiarism: the author does not publish the work of another under his own name; he publishes his work under the name of someone else" (VanderKam, *Dead Sea Scrolls Today*, 36). To our knowledge, three pseudepigrapha are attested at Qumran—*Enoch, Jubilees,* and the *Testament of the Twelve Patriarchs.*

18. For an English translation of these texts and others belonging to the same category, see Florentino García Martínez, *The*

*Dead Sea Scrolls Translated: The Qumran Texts in English* (Leiden: E. J. Brill, 1994), passim; and Vermes, *The Dead Sea Scrolls in English*, passim. On the question of whether these books were considered to be authoritative by the Qumranites, see VanderKam, *Dead Sea Scrolls Today*, 153–7, and Schiffman, *Reclaiming the Dead Sea Scrolls*, 162–7.

19. The best treatment on the subject is by Carmel McCarthy, *The Tiqqune Sopherim and Other Theological Corrections in the Masoretic Text of the Old Testament* (Göttingen: Vandenhoeck and Ruprecht, 1981), who does not limit the scribal errors to eighteen, but discusses several additional errors. See also Christian D. Ginsburg, *Introduction to the Massoretico-Critical Edition of the Hebrew Bible* (London: Trinitarian Bible Society, 1897; reprinted with prolegomenon by Harry M. Orlinsky, New York: Ktav, 1966), 352–61; and P. Kyle McCarter Jr., *Textual Criticism: Recovering the Text of the Hebrew Bible* (Philadelphia: Fortress Press, 1986), 58.

20. VanderKam, *Dead Sea Scrolls Today*, 125.

21. Emanuel Tov, *Textual Criticism of Hebrew Bible* (Minneapolis: Fortress Press, 1992), 94.

22. Ibid.

23. James A. Sanders, "Understanding the Development of the Biblical Text," in *The Dead Sea Scrolls after Forty Years*, ed. Hershel Shanks et al. (Washington, D. C.: Biblical Archaeology Society, 1991), 61.

24. Bart D. Ehrman, *The Orthodox Corruption of Scripture: The Effect of Early Christological Controversies on the Text of the New Testament* (Oxford: Oxford Univeristy Press, 1993), 43 n. 108.

25. Jack P. Lewis, *The English Bible From KJV to NIV: A History and Evaluation* (Grand Rapids, Mich.: Baker Book, 1982), 37–8, lists dozens of other details and examples of textual differences between English translations of the Bible.

26. The scholar's name was William Kilburne. See ibid.

27. *Teachings of the Prophet Joseph Smith*, comp. Joseph Fielding Smith (Salt Lake City: Deseret Book, 1938), 327.

28. See Ellis R. Brotzman, *Old Testament Textual Criticism: A Practical Introduction* (Grand Rapids, Mich.: Baker Book, 1994),

108, for examples of errors. The state of the problem of errors in the MT is summarized in the preface to the first printing of the New English Bible: "The Hebrew text as thus handed down [by the Massoretes] is full of errors of every kind due to defective archetypes and successive copyists' errors, confusion of letters, omissions and insertions, displacements of words and even whole sentences or paragraphs; and copyists' unhappy attempts to rectify mistakes have only increased the confusion" (Harold Scanlin, *The Dead Sea Scrolls and Modern Translations of the Old Testament* [Wheaton, Ill.: Tyndale, 1993], 31).

29. McCarter, *Textual Criticism*, 77–8.

30. William Hugh Brownlee, *The Meaning of the Qumran Scrolls for the Bible: With Special Attention to the Book of Isaiah* (New York: Oxford University Press, 1964), 156–7.

31. For a complete discussion of this missing verse of scripture, see Frank Moore Cross Jr., "The Ammonite Oppression of the Tribes of Gad and Reuben: Missing Verses from 1 Samuel 11 Found in 4QSamuel[a]," in *History, Historiography and Interpretation: Studies in Biblical and Cuneiform Literatures*, ed. H. Tadmor and M. Weinfeld (Jerusalem: Magnes, 1983), 148–58; and Tov, *Textual Criticism of Hebrew Bible*, 342–3.

32. Josephus refers to this incident of King Nahash in *Antiquities*, trans. H. Thackeray and R. Marcus, Loeb Classical Library, 6.68–71.

33. Translation is by the author.

34. The DSS Samuel texts (4QSam[a] and 4QSam[b]) will be published by Frank Moore Cross of Harvard University and Donald W. Parry in *Discoveries in the Judaean Desert*, vol. 17.

35. See McCarter, *Textual Criticism*, 57–61.

36. See Tov, *Textual Criticism of Hebrew Bible*, 127–8.

37. Ibid., 267–9.

38. I note, however, that not all religious texts prefer *Elohim*. For the author(s) of Proverbs, *Jehovah* is the preferred name, used scores of times against the epithet *Elohim*, which is found three times only. In addition, it is clear that the name *Jehovah* was the preference of divine names for the Elephantine Jews and was

used in its absolute state as well as in a host of theophoric names. See Bezalel Porten, *Archives from Elephantine* (Berkeley: University of California Press, 1968), 134–45. Porten asserts that "El is completely absent from the Elephantine onomasticon" (p. 135).

39. M. H. Segal, "El, Elohim, and YHWH in the Bible," *Jewish Quarterly Review* 46 (October 1955): 100. Similarly, Alexander Rofé detects that the author(s) of Chronicles omits the title *Sebaoth* in "three otherwise verbatim quotations from Samuel (1 Chronicles 13:6; 16:2; 17:25)" (Alexander Rofé, "The Name YHWH Sebaoth and the Shorter Recension of Jeremiah," in *Prophetie und geschichtliche Wirklichkeit im alten Israel. Festschrift für Siegfried Herrmann*, ed. Herausgegeben von R. Liwak and S. Wagner [Stuttgart: W. Kohlhammer, 1991], 309).

40. "The preponderance of Elohim in those psalms cannot be original," states Segal in "El, Elohim, and YHWH in the Bible" (see pp. 94, 104–5), because the psalmist would not have employed the awkward expressions *Elohim my Elohim* (Psalm 43:4) and *Elohim your Elohim* (Psalm 45:8). On the Elohistic Psalms, see also G. H. Parke-Taylor, *Yahweh: The Divine Name in the Bible* (Waterloo, Ontario: Wilfred Laurier University Press, 1975), 8–9; G. F. Moore, *Judaism I* (Cambridge: Harvard University Press, 1930), 424; G. F. Moore, *Judaism III* (Cambridge: Harvard University Press, 1930), 127; cf. Patrick W. Skehan, "The Divine Name at Qumran, in the Masada Scroll, and in the Septuagint," *Bulletin of the International Organization for Septuagint and Cognate Studies* 13 (1980): 20.

41. See Skehan, "Divine Name," 20; Robert Gordis, *Poets, Prophets, and Sages: Essays in Biblical Interpretation* (Bloomington: Indiana University Press, 1971), 167.

42. See Parke-Taylor, *Yahweh: The Divine Name in the Bible*, 8; Segal, "El, Elohim, and YHWH," 101.

43. The Song of Songs is not divinely inspired poetry; we would not necessarily expect to find the name of God there.

44. See Skehan, "Divine Name," 20–1; Gordis, *Poets, Prophets, and Sages*, 167.

45. Segal, "El, Elohim, and YHWH," 100.

46. Notable variant readings of divine names also exist in

other Samuel texts discovered in Cave 4 at Qumran. For instance, see the reading of 4QSam[b] at 1 Samuel 23:10.

47. See Donald W. Parry, "4QSam[a] and the Tetragrammaton," in *Current Research and Technological Developments,* ed. Parry and Ricks, 106–25.

48. Specifically, the Hebrew Bible lacks the Tetragrammaton on two occasions against 4QSam[a] and the Old Greek Bible, which both read *Jehovah* (see 1 Samuel 2:10; 6:20); the Hebrew Bible prefers *Elohim* on six occasions against 4QSam[a] and the Old Greek Bible, which prefer *Jehovah* (see 1 Samuel 2:25; 6:5; 10:26; 23:14; 23:16; 2 Samuel 6:3); the Hebrew Bible (and the Old Greek) omits the Tetragrammaton on three occasions that 4QSam[a] reads it (see 1 Samuel 1:22; 5:11; 11:9); in addition, in the phrase *Jehovah, the God of Israel* attested in 1 Samuel 6:3 (4QSam[a], Old Greek), the Hebrew Bible lacks the Tetragrammaton with the reading *the God of Israel.*

49. See Scanlin, *Dead Sea Scrolls and Modern Translations,* 26.

50. See ibid., 34.

51. Ibid., 27.

# CHAPTER 3

# IS THE PLAN OF SALVATION ATTESTED IN THE DEAD SEA SCROLLS?

*Dana M. Pike*

The original working title of this paper was "The Qumran Community: Where Did It Come From? Why Was It There? and Where Was It Going?" This proved not only to be somewhat cumbersome, but also misleading. Some readers would have thought that the paper focused on the origins of the Qumran community, and would have expected a discussion of theories on how these people had gathered from Jerusalem and other Judean locales, and why they had chosen a rather desolate spot on the northwest shore of the Dead Sea to live. The question Where was it going? could be answered easily: nowhere. Those at Qumran who did not escape the Roman army as it made its way along the western shore of the Dead Sea about A.D. 68 were captured or killed. However, that is not the focus here. Those three questions were intended to communicate that the intent of

*Dana M. Pike is assistant professor of ancient scripture at Brigham Young University.*

this paper is to consider evidence of the plan of salvation in the Dead Sea Scrolls.

For Latter-day Saints, the plan of salvation consists of all the principles, powers, and ordinances necessary for the children of God to return to his presence and enjoy eternal life. It is our belief that "all human beings—male and female—are created in the image of God. Each is a beloved spirit son or daughter of heavenly parents, and, as such, each has a divine nature and destiny. . . . In the premortal realm, spirit sons and daughters knew and worshipped God as their Eternal Father and accepted His plan by which His children could obtain a physical body and gain earthly experience to progress toward perfection and ultimately re-alize his or her divine destiny as an heir of eternal life."[1] This, of course, is all made possible by the redeeming sacri-fice of Jesus Christ, the first begotten of God in premortality and the Only Begotten Son of God in the flesh.[2]

Having so stated, and at the risk of eliminating all the suspense, let me now answer the question posed in the title of this paper: "Is the Plan of Salvation Attested in the Dead Sea Scrolls?" From a Latter-day Saint perspective, the an-swer is a definite no. However, if we ask, "Are there any concepts attested in the Dead Sea Scrolls that are *similar* to any of the components of the plan of salvation?," then the answer is a *qualified* yes. To understand the reason for quali-fying the answer to this second question is to understand the relationship between Latter-day Saint doctrine and practice and anything contained in the Dead Sea Scrolls. The Qumran community, generally accepted as being most closely related to a group known as the Essenes, were part of the larger group of Israelites, or Jews as we often call them, living in Judea at the turn of the era. From a Latter-day Saint perspective, the Jews as a people, including those Jews living at Qumran, were living in at least a partial state of apostasy during the last few centuries B.C. and into the new Christian era (A.D.).[3] Therefore, on the one hand, we should not expect to find pure forms of theological concepts or practices attested in the Dead Sea Scrolls and other documents of this time period. However, we should not be surprised, on the other hand, to find what I refer to as "corrupted echoes" of true doctrines and practices preserved in these documents, since these people were heirs to the prophetic legacy that is partially preserved in the Hebrew Bible (the Christian Old Testament). Although the Qumran community had separated themselves from what they considered to be corrupt Jewish authorities in Jerusalem and were anticipating and preparing themselves for the coming of a messiah or messiahs,[4] it is clear that they were not a divinely legitimized community of saints with a complete or accurate understanding of who the true Messiah was and what conditions would prevail at his first coming.[5]

Having provided this orientation, it is of interest to note that some of these people's ideas relating to the plan of salvation have a certain ring to them that Latter-day Saints can perhaps appreciate more than Jews or traditional Christians today. My paper contains examples of such ideas that relate to the three major phases of our existence: premortal life, mortality, and the afterlife. I have chosen a few representative examples of echoes of the plan of salvation that I think will be of interest.

Two points need to be made, however, before proceeding. First, it must be understood that the contents of the scrolls, as is the case with much of our own scriptural records, do not contain a developed, systematic discussion of their authors' views on any subjects. Our understanding of the Qumran community's views is based on mining nuggets of information from all of the appropriate documents. Since our understanding is dependent on what material has been preserved and discovered, it may not be completely accurate. Second, it must not be assumed that every text discovered at Qumran imparts a clear picture of what this particular community believed. Hundreds of scrolls were brought to Qumran, but only those that are thought to have been composed by members of this community are of value for this study. Therefore, I have only employed so-called sectarian texts, those documents indigenous to the Qumran community, as sources of information. Most of the passages included in this presentation are derived from the most significant sectarian scrolls from Qumran: the *Rule of the Community* (1QS), the *Thanksgiving Hymns* (1QH) and the *War Scroll* (1QM). I will now review passages relating to premortal life, the purpose of mortality, and resurrection and afterlife.

## Premortal Life and Predestination

Because these documents developed out of the biblical tradition, many passages in the sectarian documents indicate that God is the great creator who knows all things and has power over all things. Consider these three examples:

before your {God's} might, nothing is strong,
and nothing is [comparable] to your glory,
and to your wisdom there is no measure,
and your fait[hfulness has no end]

(1QH XVII [9] 16–7)[6]

Who (is) like you, God of Israel,
in the heavens or on the earth,
to do great deeds like your deeds,
marvels like your feats?

(1QM X 8)

From the God of knowledge stems all there is and all there shall be. (1QS III 15)

Thus, the God of Israel is over all and nothing can compare with his matchless power and knowledge.

Josephus, the first century A.D. Jewish historian, indicated that the Essenes believed in the premortal existence of souls, or spirits. He records that:

> their doctrine is this, that bodies are corruptible . . . but that the souls are immortal and continue for ever: and that they came out of the most subtle air, and are united to their bodies as to prisons . . . but that when they are set free from the bonds of the flesh, they then, as released from a long bondage, rejoice and mount upward. And this is like the opinion of the Greeks.[7]

While the record of Josephus cannot be used without some critical evaluation (for example, it is not clear to what extent this passage is tinged with the influence of Greek ideas), it is clear from various other sources that at least some Jews and Christians living at the turn of the era believed in the existence of spirits before these spirits entered their mortal bodies.[8] Two passages from the *Thanksgiving Hymns* strongly suggest this same idea:

> These are those you fou[nded before] the centuries,
> to judge through them all your works before creating
>       them,
> together with the host of your spirits and the assembly of
>       [the gods,]
> with the holy vault and all its hosts,
> with the earth and all its produce.
>
> (1QH V [13] 13–5)
>
> you {God} are prince of gods and king of the glorious
>       ones,
> lord of every spirit, owner of every creature
>
> (1QH XVIII [10] 8)[9]

While the inhabitants of Qumran apparently believed in the premortal existence of spirits, there is nothing in the Dead

Sea Scrolls that indicates the nature or characteristics of these spirits. They are never described as the "children" of God.

The Old Testament contains various passages that are understood by Latter-day Saints to indicate that the Lord knows "the end from the beginning" (Isaiah 46:10), and that the house of Israel (Isaiah 49:1–3) and the prophet Jeremiah (Jeremiah 1:5), for example, were called, or foreordained, from the womb or even earlier to do God's will. There are several passages in the sectarian scrolls, however, that clearly indicate that the Qumran community went beyond such conceptions of foreordination to believing in predestination—that everything in life happened according to God's will and plan. Consider the following two representative passages from the scrolls:

> In your wisdom you es[tablished] eternal [. . .];
> before creating them you know all their deeds
> for ever and ever. [. . .]
> [Without you] nothing is done,
> and nothing is known without your will.
> You have fashioned every spirit
> and [. . .]
> and the judgment of all their deeds.
> *Blank*
> You have stretched out the heavens for your glory.
> Everything [which it contains you have established] ac-
> cording to your approval. . . .
> And in the wisdom of your knowledge
> you have determined their course
> before they came to exist.
> And with [your approval] everything happens,
> and without you nothing occurs.
>
> (1QH IX [1] 7–10, 19–20)

From the God of knowledge stems all there is and all there shall be. Before they existed he made all their plans

> and when they came into being they will execute all their
> works in compliance with his instructions, according to
> his glorious design without altering anything. (1QS III
> 15–16)[10]

Based on these and similar passages, it is evident that the
inhabitants of Qumran believed more strongly in the determining power of God's foreknowledge than is evidenced in
any other Jewish writings known to us from that time period. This view roughly correlates with the statement of
Josephus that "the sect of the Essenes . . . declares that Fate
is mistress of all things, and that nothing befalls men unless
it be in accordance with her decree."[11] The passage from the
*Rule of the Community* continues:

> In his {God's} hand are the laws of all things and he sup-
> ports them in all their needs. He created man to rule the
> world and placed within him two spirits so that he
> would walk with them until the moment of his visitation:
> they are the spirits of truth and of deceit. In the hand of
> the Prince of Lights is dominion over all the sons of jus-
> tice; they walk in paths of light. And in the hand of the
> Angel of Darkness is total dominion over the sons of de-
> ceit; they walk on paths of darkness. Due to the Angel of
> Darkness all the sons of justice stray, and all their sins,
> their iniquities, their failings and their mutinous deeds
> are under his dominion in compliance with the mysteries
> of God, until his moment; and all their punishments and
> their periods of grief are caused by the dominion of his
> enmity; and all the spirits of their lot cause the sons of
> light to fall. However, the God of Israel and the angel of
> his truth assist all the sons of light. He created the spirits
> of light and of darkness and on them established all his
> deeds. (1QS III 16–25)[12]

This passage indicates that God created two spirits, the
Prince of Lights and the Angel of Darkness, who each have

their "lot" or group of spirit followers that influence people with "truth" or "deceit." Latter-day Saints may see in this the aftermath of the war in heaven. That may well be the origin of this concept at Qumran, but it must be pointed out that in the Qumran material there is no mention of such a war, nor of a loss of status for the Angel of Darkness.[13] Note also that in the preceding passage the Angel of Darkness is described as being created evil by God. While it might be tempting to suggest that the Qumran community did not really believe in predestination, but in foreordination, thus allowing for an individual's agency, similar to the Latter-day Saint conception, I do not see how the passages just cited can be understood to indicate anything other than predestination.

There is, however, another dimension to this picture. There are several passages, especially in the *Thanksgiving Hymns*, that seem to suggest that in the doctrines taught at Qumran there was a certain amount of free will or agency that people could exercise in order to merit God's grace and forgiveness. For example:

> Dread and dismay have gripped me . . .
> for I have remembered my faults . . .
> But when I remembered the strength of your hand
> and the abundance of your compassion
> I remained resolute and stood up . . .
> for you have supported me by your kindnesses
> and by you abundant compassion.
> Because you atone for sin
> and cle[anse man] of his fault through your justice.
> (1QH XII [4] 33–7)

> All the sons of your truth
> /you take/ to forgiveness in your presence,
> you purify them from their sins

by the greatness of your goodness,
and in your bountiful mercy.

(1QH XV [7] 30)

In his compassion he draws me near,
and in his mercy he brings my judgment.
In the righteousness of his truth he judges me.
In his great goodness he atones for all my iniquities.
In his righteousness he cleanses me.

(1QS XI 13–4)[14]

Space does not allow a full exploration of how these concepts—predestination, agency, and forgiveness—could comfortably coexist in the thought of the Qumran community. E. H. Merrill has observed, "the very fact that a man joined the Community proved that he was one of the predestined. He did not do so to become one of the Elect; he did so because he was one of the Elect. Predestination did not contradict free will; it provided the rationale as to why men chose 'freely' as they did."[15] From the perspective of the inhabitants of Qumran, those who entered the covenant of the community and remained faithful in that covenant as true Israel had been predestined to be the elect of God. Yes, they would sin and need to be forgiven, but this like everything else, happened because God had willed it long ago.

In summary, the Qumran sectarian scrolls indicate that God created all things, including good and evil spirits, as well as the spirits or souls of people before they existed in the flesh, and that God determined which people would be saved and which people would be destroyed.[16] These passages suggest to me corrupted echoes of the war in heaven and of God's foreordination of his spirit children, concepts that Latter-day Saints believe were known and understood in previous gospel dispensations. However, by the time of the Qumran community it appears that their understanding was well off the track of true doctrine.[17]

# The Purpose of Mortality

Latter-day Saints understand that mortality is a significant stage in our eternal progression. When asked about the purpose of mortality, a Latter-day Saint will often respond with a statement similar to this one:

> There came a time [in our premortal existence] when . . . we were taught that we would come down here for two purposes: first, to gain bodies, mortal bodies, which would be given us again in immortality, in a resurrected state, as a consequence of an infinite and eternal atoning sacrifice which would be made; and secondly, that we would come here to be examined and tried and tested, to see if we would believe the truth, accept the truth, live the truth, walk in conformity to the mind and will of the Lord, as that was revealed to us by his prophets.[18]

The classic scriptural statement on the purpose of mortality is in the book of Abraham:

> And there stood one among them that was like unto God, and he said unto those who were with him: We will go down, for there is space there, and we will take of these materials, and we will make an earth whereon these may dwell; And we will prove them herewith, to see if they will do all things whatsoever the Lord their God shall command them; And they who keep their first estate shall be added upon; and they who keep not their first estate shall not have glory in the same kingdom with those who keep their first estate; and they who keep their second estate shall have glory added upon their heads for ever and ever. (Abraham 3:24–6)

These and other passages emphasize that there is a divine purpose to our mortal existence and that the acquisition of a physical body is essential to our progress. However, this idea of mortality as a second stage of development, which follows the opportunity we had for progression in our premortal existence, appears to be totally absent from the Dead Sea Scrolls. While members of the Qumran community seem to have believed in the existence of spirits before mortality, I am not aware of any passage in the scrolls that indicates the community's view of why spirits come to earth. Furthermore, there are no passages that indicate that receiving a physical, mortal body is a positive step. Again, it could be argued that our information is incomplete, but if the statement by Josephus that the Essenes viewed mortal bodies as "prisons" from which spirits are glad to be released at death is accurate, then it is not surprising that passages contradicting that view are not attested in the scrolls.

Similarly, there is no specific indication in the Dead Sea Scrolls of the idea that mortality is a training and testing period. However, as we might expect to find in the records of a community grounded on a particular interpretation of the Hebrew Bible, there is ample evidence that faithfulness to God's will was extremely important. Consider the opening lines of the *Rule of the Community* which express in general terms the expected commitment from those who wished to enter this covenant community:

> In order to seek God with [all the heart and soul] doing what is good and right before him, as he commanded Moses and through all his servants the prophets, and in order to love all that he has chosen, and to hate all that he has rejected, keeping away from all evil and adhering to all good works, and in order to perform truth and righteousness and justice upon the earth; to walk no longer with the stubbornness of a guilty heart, and (no longer with) lustful eyes doing all evil; in order to receive all those who devote themselves to do the statutes of God into the covenant of mercy, to be joined to the Council of God, to walk perfectly before him (according to) all

revealed (laws) at their appointed times, and in order to love all the Sons of Light each according to his lot in the Council of God, and to hate all the Sons of Darkness each according to his guilt at the vengeance of God; all those devoting themselves to his truth bringing all their knowledge, and their strength, and their property into the Community of God in order to strengthen their knowledge by the truth of God's statues, and discipline their strength according to the perfection of his ways, and all their property according to his righteous counsel, and in order not to deviate from any single one of all the commands of God in their times, . . . thus all those who are entering shall cross over into the covenant before God by the Rule of the Community, in order to act according to everything which he has commanded. They must not turn back from following after him because of any terror, dread, affliction, or agony during the reign of Belial.[19]

Similar thoughts, less extensively developed, are also attested in other sectarian scrolls, such as these in the *Thanksgiving Hymns*:

{I will} look for the spirit [. . .]
to be strengthened by the spirit of holiness,
to adhere to the truth of your covenant,
to serve you in truth, with a perfect heart,
to love your [will.]

(1QH VIII [16] 14–5)

with an oath I have enjoined my soul
not to sin against you
and not to do anything which is evil in your eyes.

(1QH VI [14] 17–8)

Thus, those who entered into this covenant group at Qumran were expected both to know and do God's will as it was understood by the community. Sentiments such as "not to sin against you and not to do anything which is evil in your eyes" are attested elsewhere in the Dead Sea Scrolls, suggesting the strict nature of obedience expected in this covenant group.

Several passages, especially in the *Thanksgiving Hymns*, indicate that these people felt the need for divine assistance as they tried to strictly observe their covenant obligations. Consider these representative statements:

> I give thanks, Lord,
> because you have sustained me with your strength,
> you have spread your holy spirit over me so that I will
> not stumble,
> and you have fortified me against the wars of wickedness.
>
> (1QH XV [7] 6–7)

> What will I say if you do not open my mouth?
> How can I understand if you do not teach me?
> What can I purpose if you do not open my heart?
> How will I walk on the right path
> if you do not steady [my feet?]
> How will my step stay secure
> [if you do not] strengthen [me] with strength?
>
> (1QH XX [12] 33–5)

Both the need for obedience to God's will and the importance of God's strength to assist one in being faithful to him finds rich expression in the Hebrew Bible and in these and other passages from the Dead Sea Scrolls.

We must again note, however, that several passages from the scrolls cited above indicate that these people believed that God had predestined certain people to be faithful and thus to be saved. According to this view, those who were obedient to God's will had already been designated by God to be so. This perspective alone distances the Latter-day Saint view of the nature and purpose of mortality from what is attested at Qumran.

Given the silence in the scrolls concerning the relationship between premortal spirits and God, no indication of a positive attitude about gaining a mortal body, and the concept that obedience is a consequence of predestination and not an indication of faithfully exercised agency, it seems clear that the purpose and significance of mortality as understood by Latter-day Saints is nowhere to be found in the documents from Qumran.

## Resurrection and Afterlife

There are several statements relating to salvation in the sectarian documents, especially in the *Thanksgiving Hymns*. However, most of these passages are vague at best concerning what the inhabitants of Qumran really understood about the afterlife. Even though some Jews at the turn of the era, especially the Pharisees, believed in the physical resurrection of the body,[20] there is no unambiguous statement of the doctrine of resurrection in Qumran texts that are clearly sectarian. The following passage may be understood to suggest a belief in resurrection:

> For your glory, you have purified man from sin,
> so that he can make himself holy for you . . .
> and {be} in the lot of your holy ones,
> to raise the worms of the dead
> from the dust, to an [everlasting] community
> and from a depraved spirit, to your knowledge
> so that he can take his place in your presence
> with the perpetual host
> and the [everlasting] spirits,
> to renew him with everything that will exist.
>
> (1QH XIX [11] 10–3)

If the inhabitants of Qumran believed in a literal resurrection I would expect a more specific statement than the passage just cited. Perhaps the statement from Josephus quoted earlier is accurate: "when they [people's spirits or souls] are set free from the bonds of the flesh, they then, as released from a long bondage, rejoice and mount upward."[21] However, in contrast to this, we have a statement from Hippolytus, a leader in the Christian church at Rome about A.D. 200, who stated that "the doctrine of the resurrection of the dead has also derived support among [the Essenes], for they acknowledge both that the flesh will rise again, and that it will be immortal, in the same manner that the soul is already imperishable."[22] We cannot yet confidently determine which one of these descriptions is correct.

A text discovered in Cave 4 of Qumran, designated 4Q521, strongly suggests a belief in resurrection:

> The Lord will perform marvelous acts such as have not existed, just as he sa[id], for he will heal the badly wounded and will make the dead live, he will proclaim good news to the meek, give lavishly [to the need]y, lead the exiled and enrich the hungry. (4Q521 2, ii, 11–3)[23]

A second reference to resurrection may be seen on another fragment of this same text (5, ii, 6–7): "[. . .] like these, the accursed. And they shall be for death, [when he makes] the dead of his people [ri]se." It is not clear, however, that this text is indigenous to the Qumran group, so it is difficult to know to what extent it represents the thought of the community.

Many writings that contain references to the condition of the righteous in the afterlife focus on praising God for his goodness and power. Consider these two passages from the *Hymns*:

> The corrupt spirit you have purified
> from the great sin
> so that he can take his place
> with the host of the holy ones,
> and can enter in communion
> with the congregation of the sons of heaven.

You cast eternal destiny for man
with the spirits of knowledge,
so that he praises your name together in celebration,
and tells of your wonders before all your works.

(1QH XI [3] 21–3)[24]

All the sons of your truth
/you take/ to forgiveness in your presence,
you purify them from their sins
by the greatness of your goodness,
and in your bountiful mercy,
to make them stand in your presence,
for ever and ever.

(1QH XV [7] 30–1)

Perhaps the most interesting passage relating to the afterlife is found in the *Rule of the Community*:

These are the counsels of the spirit for the sons of truth in the world. And the visitation of those who walk in it will be for healing, plentiful peace in a long life, fruitful offspring with all everlasting blessings, eternal enjoyment with endless life, and a crown of glory with majestic raiment in eternal light. (1QS IV 6–8)[25]

While these passages provide a general but glowing picture of a future existence for those predestined to enjoy such, there is no specific mention of the opportunities inherent in a Latter-day Saint understanding of exaltation.

The wicked, of course, could not expect to enjoy such pleasing conditions. Several passages in the sectarian scrolls speak of the destruction of the wicked at the end of the world (see, for example, 1QH XIV [6] 29–32 and 1QpHab XIII 2–4), although these contribute little to our attempt to understand their view of the afterlife. There is one passage in the *Rule of the Community*, however, that vividly describes the fate of the wicked in the world to come:

The visitation of all those who walk in it {the Spirit of Deceit} (will be) many afflictions by all the angels of punishment, eternal perdition by the fury of God's vengeful wrath, everlasting terror and endless shame, together with disgrace of annihilation in the fire of the dark region. And all their times for their generations (will be expended) in dreadful suffering and bitter misery in dark abysses until they are destroyed. (There will be) no remnant nor rescue for them. (1QS IV 11–4)[26]

While it is not clear to me how "eternal perdition" and "annihilation" can coexist, it is possible that the torment suffered by the wicked in the "dark region" mentioned in this passage is a corrupted echo of the Latter-day Saint concept of outer darkness to which sons of perdition will be banished.

Taken together, these and other passages from the sectarian scrolls mentioning life after death do not provide us with much specific information other than the view that the righteous may be resurrected and will be happy praising God in glorious conditions and that the wicked will suffer endlessly or, perhaps, be annihilated.

Again, it is important for our purposes to understand that there is no mention in the sectarian scrolls of degrees of glory in the afterlife, nor of a personal Savior, nor a great redemptive sacrifice, or related concepts as taught in Isaiah 53, in the New Testament, and in the Book of Mormon. Additionally, there is no mention that the concept of the messiah as taught at Qumran involves the Son of God in the sense that Latter-day Saints understand it.

## Summary and Conclusion

I hope that this brief review of the Qumran community's concepts of premortal, mortal, and postearth life has illustrated some of the interesting content of the sectarian scrolls from Qumran and has illustrated some of the difficulties that exist in understanding the ideas contained in them. Our relative uncertainty of the details of many of their conceptions only complicates the difficulties of relating them to Latter-day Saint doctrine.

I feel strongly that Latter-day Saints can appreciate and understand the passages in the Dead Sea Scrolls that relate to the plan of salvation, but we must also appreciate that a clear or comprehensive understanding of this plan is not evidenced at Qumran. Though there are concepts that I have described as corrupted echoes of true doctrines, there are simply too many key points of the plan of salvation absent from the preserved texts. Doctrines such as the fall, the infinite atonement of the Savior, clear indications of a universal, physical resurrection, and eternal ordinances requiring the holy Melchizedek Priesthood are not attested. The Dead Sea Scrolls cannot teach Latter-day Saints anything about the plan of salvation that has not already been revealed by the Lord through his authorized servants. However, our study of the scrolls can help us to understand the beliefs of the Jewish inhabitants of Qumran and, because of the contrasts, such study can help us more fully appreciate the gospel truths restored in the latter days.

## Notes

I wish to thank Becky Schulties for her assistance in the preparation of this paper.

1. The First Presidency and the Council of the Twelve Apostles of The Church of Jesus Christ of Latter-day Saints, "The Family: A Proclamation to the World," *Ensign* (November 1995): 102. See also Moses 6:55–62 and other scriptural passages as listed in the Topical Guide, s.v. "salvation, plan of."

2. See, for example, Romans 8:29; Hebrews 1:6; 2 Nephi 25:12; Moses 1:6.

3. Those Jews who accepted the declarations of Jesus represent a significant exception to this statement, of course. However, the statement is made as a general observation on the status of all Jews at the end of the old era and most Jews at the beginning of the new one, the time when the Qumran community was in existence.

4. See the discussion of the messianic concept at Qumran by Florentino García Martínez in this volume.

5. Reasons that the inhabitants of Qumran *cannot* be viewed as so-called primitive Christians anticipating the true Messiah include: they seem to have believed in multiple messianic figures with different functions, especially royal and priestly functions (i.e., from a Latter-day Saint perspective, they fragmented the various roles of the true Messiah among separate individuals); their messiahs were not imagined to be divine; their messiahs would come with power and bring a new order to the earth (not unlike what we expect Jesus to do at his second coming), but they would live the pure form of the law of Moses after the coming of their messiahs; these people made no claims to be prophets authorized to speak for the Lord; and there is no prophetic reference in the Scrolls to Jesus or John the Baptist, whose names had been prophesied long before this time according to Latter-day Saint belief, nor is there any mention of John the Baptist or any of the apostles who actually ministered the gospel during the last three decades of the community's existence at Qumran.

6. All English renditions of passages from the Dead Sea Scrolls in this paper are quoted from Florentino García Martínez, trans., *The Dead Sea Scrolls Translated*, translated into English by Wilfred G. E. Watson (Leiden: E. J. Brill, 1994), unless otherwise noted. Note also that the columns of the scroll containing the *Thanksgiving Hymns* (1QH) have been renumbered since they were originally published. García Martínez uses this more recent numeration. I have provided the older numeration in brackets for convenience in using other translations, such as the one by Vermes.

7. Josephus, *Wars of the Jews*, ed. E. H. Warmington (London: William Heinemann, 1921), II.8.11.

8. See, for example, *2 Enoch* 23:4–5 in *The Old Testament Pseudepigrapha*, ed. James H. Charlesworth (Garden City, N.Y.: Doubleday, 1983), 1:140, and Hebrews 12:9.

9. Interestingly, the title *Lord of Spirits* is used several times in the Jewish pseudepigraphic text *1 Enoch*, which dates from about the time of the Qumran community but was not composed by it. See *1 Enoch* II.37–71 in *Old Testament Pseudepigrapha*, ed. Charlesworth, 1:29–50.

10. These and other passages, including CD II 2–13 and 1QpHab VII 5–15, are briefly reviewed by Armin Lange, "Wisdom and Predestination in the Dead Sea Scrolls," *Dead Sea Discoveries* 2/3 (1995): 340–54.

11. Josephus, *Antiquities of the Jews*, trans. Ralph Marcus, Loeb Classical Library (1943), 13.172f.

12. Note the similar perception preserved in 1QM XIII 9–13: "You, [have crea]ted [us] for you, eternal people, and you have made us fall into the lot of light in accordance with your truth. From of old you appointed the Prince of light to assist us, and in [. . .] and all the spirits of truth are under his dominion. You created Belial for the pit, angel of enmity; his [dom]ain is darkness, his counsel is for evil and wickedness. All the spirits of his lot angels of destruction walk in the laws of darkness; towards them goes his only desire. We, instead, in the lot of your truth, rejoice in your mighty hand, we exult in your salvation, we are happy with your aid and your peace. Who is like you in strength, God of Israel?" See also CD II 7–10.

13. Elsewhere in the scrolls and other Jewish literature of the period the chief wicked spirit is designated as Belial, a title for Satan that occurs once in the New Testament (2 Corinthians 2:16). Greek manuscripts of this verse actually read *Beliar*, a common variant of *Belial* in Rabbinic and pseudepigraphic documents.

14. Elisha Qimron and James H. Charlesworth, trans., *Rule of the Community and Related Documents*, vol. 1 of *The Dead Sea*

*Scrolls,* ed. James H. Charlesworth (Louisville: Westminster John Knox, 1994), 49.

15. Eugene H. Merrill, *Qumran and Predestination: A Theological Study of the Thanksgiving Hymns* (Leiden: E. J. Brill, 1975), 58.

16. Latter-day Saints may remember that a similar belief of predestination is evident in the account of the apostate Zoramites' prayer (see Alma 31:17).

17. Another passage in 1QM X 11–5 indicates that as part of his plan, God not only decided the fate of individuals, but of nations: "[. . . You created] . . . the earth and the laws of its divisions in desert and steppe, of all its products . . . of beast and birds, of man's image, of the gener[ations of . . .], of the division of tongues, of the separation of peoples, of the dwelling of the clans, of the legacy of nations. . . ." (compare Acts 17:26).

18. Bruce R. McConkie, "The New and Everlasting Covenant of Marriage," *BYU Speeches of the Year* (Provo, Utah: BYU Harold B. Lee Library, 1960), 3.

19. *Rule of the Community* (1QS) I 1–18, in Qimron and Charlesworth, *Rule of the Community,* 7–9. Note the emphasis on loving the faithful "sons of light" and hating the "sons of darkness." Since such a concept is not found in the Hebrew Bible or rabbinic writings, it is often suggested that this teaching, found in several passages in the sectarian scrolls, may have served as the background for Jesus' statement that "ye have heard that it hath been said, Thou shalt love thy neighbor and hate thine enemy. But I say unto you, Love your enemies" (Matthew 5:43–4).

20. See Acts 23:6–9.

21. Josephus, *Wars of the Jews,* II.8.11 (2.154–5).

22. As cited in James C. VanderKam, *The Dead Sea Scrolls Today* (Grand Rapids, Mich.: Eerdmans, 1994), 79.

23. This text is also known as 4QMessianic Apocalypse. It draws on Isaiah 61:1, a scripture that was quoted in reference to Jesus in Luke 4:18.

24. Some scholars have suggested that this passage does not really refer to the afterlife, but to the conditions of members of the

community. See, for example, VanderKam, *Dead Sea Scrolls Today*, 80.

25. Interestingly, the expression "crown of glory" occurs in a similar context in 1 Peter 5:4 and D&C 104:7 (see also its occurrence in Isaiah 28:5; 62:3; and Proverbs 4:9; 16:31, and related expressions such as "crown of life" occur elsewhere in the New Testament and Doctrine and Covenants).

26. Qimron and Charlesworth, *Rule of the Community*, 17.

# CHAPTER 4

# PRAISE, PRAYER, AND WORSHIP AT QUMRAN
*David Rolph Seely*

## Biblical Worship

At the beginning of time, Adam and Eve demonstrated for their posterity the proper way to worship. They "called upon the name of the Lord" (Moses 5:4) after leaving the Garden of Eden. In response to their prayer, the voice of the Lord "gave them commandments, that they should worship the Lord their God" (Moses 5:5). Moses tells us that Adam and Eve were "obedient unto the commandments of the Lord" (Moses 5:5). They were commanded to "offer the firstlings of their flocks . . . [in] similitude of the sacrifice of the Only Begotten of the Father" (Moses 5:5, 7), to repent of their sins, and to participate in other ordinances of the gospel, namely to receive baptism and the gift of the Holy Ghost (see Moses 6:64–8). As Adam and his posterity called upon the Lord, the Lord blessed them. Moses records that a book of remembrance was kept that included inspired

*David Rolph Seely is associate professor of ancient scripture at Brigham Young University.*

writings, and Adam and Eve's children were blessed by being able to read the words contained therein (see Moses 6:5–6). And it is recorded that Adam and Eve "blessed the name of God" (Moses 5:12). These verses suggest that true worship of the Lord includes at least seven elements: (1) calling upon the Lord in prayer, (2) obedience, (3) sacrifice, (4) repentance, (5) ordinances, (6) reading and studying the word of the Lord, and (7) continuing to bless the Lord's name.

These same principles were taught to the covenant people in the law of Moses. In the books of the Pentateuch, the Lord instructs Israel in regards to worship. Israel was commanded to continue to call upon the Lord in prayer. In Deuteronomy the Lord teaches, "But if from thence thou shalt seek the Lord thy God, thou shalt find him, if thou seek him with all thy heart and with all thy soul" (Deuteronomy 4:29). In the Psalms he said, "O give thanks unto the Lord; call upon his name: . . . Seek the Lord, and his strength: seek his face evermore" (Psalms 105:1, 4). The Old Testament gives many examples of people who call upon the name of the Lord: Abraham pleads for the preservation of Sodom (see Genesis 18:23–33), Hannah gives thanks for the birth of Samuel (see 1 Samuel 2:1–10), and Solomon dedicates the temple (see 1 Kings 8:12–53). Obedience was defined as becoming "holy" as God is holy. The Lord commands in Leviticus, "Ye shall be holy: for I the Lord your God am holy" (Leviticus 19:2), and the Lord blessed Israel with many commandments to help them in their quest for holiness.

The sacrificial system was greatly expanded at the time of Moses, as delineated in the book of Leviticus, to include the sin, trespass, and peace offerings in addition to burnt offerings, as further symbols of the atonement that was to come. Israel was taught to repent with a "broken spirit:

a broken and a contrite heart" (Psalms 51:17) accompanied by sacrifices and ordinances of purification to remind them of the atonement that made repentance possible. Many ordinances in addition to circumcision, baptism, and the gift of the Holy Ghost were revealed to the children of Israel. Those ordinances included the sacrifices and rituals of purification as well as the observance of a whole series of festivals designed to help covenant Israel remember their God, their sacred history, and their covenantal relationship with him. In addition, the reading and study of the Law were legislated as a part of worship. For example, every seven years Israel was commanded to gather and read the entire Law (see Deuteronomy 31:10–2).

The Bible is replete with examples of men and women who blessed the name of the Lord, offering up hymns of praise and thanksgiving. The Psalms in particular preserve many such hymns of praise and thanksgiving.[1]

## Qumran Worship

Members of the Qumran community, understood by most scholars to be Essenes, were first and foremost Jews. They based their beliefs and practices on the Bible and other sacred books and thus they worshipped in ways similar to other Jews during this period. They believed themselves to be the only true covenant Israel, that they alone had access to the mind and the will of God, and that they had been called out of the world to prepare themselves to be ready for the end of time when they would be instruments in the hand of the Lord for the deliverance of the Sons of Light and the destruction of the Sons of Darkness.

From a historical perspective the Essenes are considered one of the several sects of Judaism, like the Pharisees and the Sadducees, that flourished at the end of the pre-Christian era. From a Latter-day Saint perspective, the Essenes were a group groping for light and truth during one of the most challenging periods of Israel's history. Although it was a time of apostasy, and darkness surrounded them, they continued to worship the Lord to the best of their ability and understanding. When Jesus the Messiah came in his mortal ministry, the Essenes as a group did not accept him. In A.D. 68 they were still at Qumran awaiting divine intervention on their behalf when their community was destroyed by the Romans.

We are fortunate to have discovered in Qumran the many texts that preserve remnants of Essene religious beliefs and practices. On the one hand, certain aspects of their worship are similar to that of the other sects of Judaism, since much of it is derived directly from the Old Testament. On the other hand, some of their beliefs and religious practices are unique to their community. We can survey their worship by examining each of the seven elements of worship identified in the Pearl of Great Price and the Bible: prayer, obedience, sacrifice, ordinances, repentance, study, and blessing the name of the Lord. For each of the seven elements I have chosen one or more representative passages from some of the important texts at Qumran to illustrate the Qumranites' understanding of each principle of worship.[2]

### Prayer at Qumran

Like all forms of Judaism based on the Bible, prayer was a very important element of the worship at Qumran. Many of the more than 800 texts found at Qumran contain prayers. The most widely attested text at Qumran is the book of Psalms, which contains examples of many prayers. There were fragments of 36 different copies of the Psalms found at Qumran, 29 copies of Deuteronomy, 21 copies of

Isaiah, and 17 copies of Exodus.[3] We now have numerous texts containing the prayers used at Qumran as well as a wealth of information about the practice of prayer. Unfortunately, many of these texts are very fragmentary. Most of the 575 texts from Cave 4 consisted of many small fragments when the Bedouin first brought them to scholars, but scholars through the years have sorted these fragments and assembled them on plates preserving, albeit in fragmentary form, hundreds of texts from Cave 4 that are useful for the study of prayer at Qumran.[4]

Qumran Cave 4, located near the ruins of Qumran, is where the remains of hundreds of biblical and other documents were found. (Photograph courtesy Melvin J. Thorne.)

The ancient historian Flavius Josephus describes for us how the Essenes prayed:

> Before the sun is up they utter no word on mundane matters, but offer to him [the Lord] certain prayers, which have been handed down from their forefathers, as though entreating him to rise. They are then dismissed by their superiors to the various crafts in which they are severally proficient and are strenuously employed until the fifth hour, when they again assemble in one place

and, after girding their loins with linen cloths, bathe their bodies in cold water. . . . Pure now themselves, they repair to the refectory as to some sacred shrine. . . . Before meat the priest says a grace, and none may partake until after the prayer.[5]

One of the treasures from Qumran is a copy of the scroll called the *Rule of the Community* (originally called the *Manual of Discipline* by scholars). This scroll contains eleven well-preserved columns discussing the rules for entrance into the community and the rituals and the ordinances and statutes governing the community. At the end of the scroll is a beautiful hymn expressing thanksgiving to the Lord for being part of the community. From this hymn we learn more about prayer at Qumran:

> When I stretch out hand and foot I will praise his name. When I go out and come in, sit and rise, and when laid on my couch, I will cry for joy to him. I will praise him with the offering of the utterance of my lips in the row of men, and before I lift my hand to enjoy the delights of the world's produce. In the beginning of terror and dread, and in the abode of affliction and distress I will bless him for (his) exceedingly woundrous activity. I will meditate upon his power, and upon his mercies I will lean all day.[6]

In short, the Essenes believed in the need to pray regularly and constantly. Prayer could be offered at any time, in any place, in any circumstance, and at Qumran there were also set times for regular prayer in the morning and in the evening. The *Rule of the Community* specifies prayer when the light of day first appears in the morning and when it disappears in the evening (See 1QS IX 26–X 3). A series of texts from Cave 4 appears to preserve specific examples of these daily prayers for each day of a month (see 4Q503). Many scholars believe that the morning and evening prayers of the Essenes were offered, as in other sects of Judaism, at the same times as the daily sacrifices at the temple in Jerusalem.[7]

Most of the prayers in the Bible appear to be spontaneous prayers directly addressing God in light of various circumstances. In the later rabbinic traditions rabbis warned against routine and unthoughtful prayer. According to the Mishnah (compiled ca. A.D. 200) Rabbi Simeon ben Nethanel said, "And when thou prayest make not thy prayer a fixed form, but [a plea for] mercies and supplications before God" (*Avot* 2:13). In rabbinic Judaism there is evidence that the writing down of prayers was not permitted during the centuries that the Essenes flourished. One of the sages stated that "those who commit blessings to writing are like those who burn Torah" (T *Shabbat* 13:4). Nevertheless, through the centuries a book of fixed prayers emerged in rabbinic Judaism.[8] Thus the Qumran prayers are important evidence for the development of prayer between the biblical period and the texts of rabbinic Judaism, which began to be written in the third century A.D. Several of the Qumran texts preserve remnants of prayers known from the rabbinic prayer book—often with the exact phrases intact—indicating that originally these prayers were known within Judaism outside of the Pharisaical circles.[9]

Undoubtedly, spontaneous prayer occurred at Qumran, and perhaps some of our texts preserve examples of such prayers. Many of the texts from Qumran appear to be fixed prayers uttered by the community on special occasions. A survey of some of the more important of the prayer texts will give us an idea of the wealth of the prayers found in the Dead Sea Scrolls.

In Cave 11 a scroll was discovered called the *Psalms Scroll*, which contains a collection of forty-one biblical

Psalms and seven non-canonical psalms, some of which are known from the Apocrypha, interspersed. Many scholars believe this scroll was a liturgical collection, meaning they were psalms used in the worship of the community.[10] At the end of this scroll was a notation of the number of hymns that David wrote:

> David son of Jesse was wise and brilliant like the light of the sun; (he was) a scribe, intelligent and perfect in all his ways before God and men.
>
> YHWH gave him an intelligent and brilliant spirit, and he wrote 3,600 psalms and 364 songs to sing before the altar for the daily perpetual sacrifice, for all the days of the year; and 52 songs for the Sabbath offerings; and 30 songs for the New Moons, for Feast days and for the Day of Atonement.
>
> In all, the songs which he uttered were 446, and 4 songs to make music on behalf of those stricken (by evil spirits).
>
> In all, they were 4,050.
>
> All these he uttered through prophecy which was given him from before the Most High.[11]

This passage confirms our suspicion that psalms were important elements in the worship of the community on a daily basis as well as throughout the yearly cycle of festivals. This passage also indicates the nature of the Qumran calendar. While we do not have Davidic psalms for each day of the year and all of the festivals, we do have fragmentary texts consisting of prayers for morning and evening of each day of the month (4Q503), prayers for various festivals (4Q507–9)—in particular the Day of Atonement (1Q34bis), a collection of prayers for the days of the week (4Q504), prayers of lamentation (4Q501), and a scroll called *Songs of the Sabbath Sacrifices* containing angelic praises of God for the first thirteen Sabbaths of the solar year (4Q400–7; 11Q5–6).

## Obedience

The *Rule of the Community* outlines the goal of the Essenes: "In order to seek God with [all the heart and soul] doing what is good and right before him, as he commanded through Moses and through all his servants the prophets, and in order to love all that he has chosen, and to hate all that he has rejected, keeping away from all evil and adher-

Qumran Cave 11, looking out toward the Dead Sea. The *Temple Scroll* and *Psalms Scroll* were discovered here. (Photograph courtesy Steven W. Booras.)

ing to all good works, and in order to perform truth and righteousness and justice upon the earth" (1QS I 1–6). The Essenes were strict about obeying the law of Moses in terms of ethics, ritual, and purification, and their books contain specific penalties imposed on those who were not obedient to the code of conduct outlined. For example, speaking the name of God frivolously and murmuring against the authority of the community were grounds for permanent expulsion from the community. Anyone who "deliberately or through negligence transgresses one word of the law of Moses, on any point whatever, shall be expelled from the

Council of the Community and shall return no more" (1QS VIII 20–25). Stiff penalties were imposed on those who spoke in anger, deceived or insulted a fellow, interrupted a meeting, or dressed immodestly (See 1QS VII 1–15). Falling asleep in the Assembly of the Congregation was punishable by penance for thirty days (See 1QS VII 10). In the *Damascus Document*, another text describing the rules of the community, there is an entire section of laws regarding proper conduct on the Sabbath (See CD X 15–XII 1).

As a symbol of their obedience, the Essenes had apparently adopted, as had other Jews, the use of the *tefillin* and *mezuzoth* as part of their worship. In Deuteronomy, in a passage Jews call the *Shemaᶜ*, which means "hear" or "hearken," the Lord commanded Israel:

> Hear, O Israel: The Lord our God is one Lord: And thou shalt love the Lord thy God with all thine heart, and with all thy soul, and with all thy might. And these words, which I command thee this day, shall be in thine heart: And thou shalt teach them [the words of the Lord] diligently unto thy children, and shalt talk of them when thou sittest in thine house, and when thou walkest by the way, and when thou liest down, and when thou risest up. And thou shall bind them for a sign upon thine hand, and they shall be as frontlets between thine eyes. And thou shalt write them upon the posts of thy house, and on thy gates. (Deuteronomy 6:4–9)

At a certain point in time pious Jews interpreted literally the passage about binding these words on the hand and before the eyes and developed objects to be used in worship called tefillin (or phylacteries) to be placed upon the hands and before the eyes, as well as the mezuzoth to be placed on the doors of their houses. Twenty tefillin and several mezuzoth were found at Qumran. The *tefillah* (singular for *tefillin*), which was placed on the forehead, had four compartments for four tiny texts containing four scriptures (Exodus 13:1–10, 11–6; Deuteronomy 6:4–9; 11:13–21). The tefillah for the hand had only one compartment for a text containing all four passages. The texts in the tefillin at Qumran include the Decalogue along with the other four traditional texts, suggesting, as do other ancient witnesses, that the recitation of the Ten Commandments was part of the liturgy, or prayer service, at Qumran. The tefillin and the mezuzoth are graphic symbols of the Essene's commitment to obedience to the Law.

### Sacrifice

The most prominent symbols connected to the law of Moses are a series of divinely ordained sacrifices. At the time of the Essenes most Jews believed, based on Deuteronomy 12, that sacrifices could only be made at the temple in Jerusalem. However, the Essenes believed that the temple in Jerusalem was being run by a corrupt and illegitimate priesthood, and therefore they apparently did not offer sacrifice there. They understood their community to be the temple of the Lord until the temple in Jerusalem could be purified and rebuilt, and they looked to the future when such a temple would be built, as described in their *Temple Scroll*. The famous *Temple Scroll* found in Cave 11 contains specific instructions for sacrifices and other temple rituals.[12]

For the Qumran community, prayer was an act that could have the same effect as sacrifice until the temple was built. The *Rule of the Community* recognizes prayer as a form of worship comparable to sacrifice: "and prayer rightly offered shall be as an acceptable fragrance of righteousness, and perfection of way as a delectable free-will offering" (1QS IX 4–5). The morning and evening prayers at Qumran were likely offered at precisely the same time as the daily sacrifices at the Jerusalem Temple.

## Ordinances and Rituals

The Essenes believed themselves to be the only true remnant of the covenant people of Israel. This is reflected in a prayer from Cave 1:

> But in the time of Thy goodwill Thou didst choose for Thyself a people. Thou didst remember Thy Covenant and [granted] that they should be set apart for Thyself from among all the peoples as a holy thing. And Thou didst renew for them Thy Covenant (founded)on a glorious vision and the words of Thy Holy [Spirit], on the works of Thy hands and the writing of Thy Right Hand, that they might know the foundations of glory and the steps toward eternity.[13]

Entrance into the covenant consisted of a ritual initiation reminiscent of the covenant ceremony described in Deuteronomy 27 to 29. The *Rule of the Community* tells us that each initiate "shall take upon his soul by a binding oath to return to the Torah of Moses, according to all which he has commanded with all heart and with all soul" (1QS V 8). As recorded in the *Rule of the Community*, entrance to the community was a complex process that consisted of several steps: an examination, a one-year conditional membership, another examination, and another year of provisional membership followed by full membership—which consisted of giving up one's private property to the community and receiving full fellowship in the community (1QS VI 13–24).

Members of the covenant participated in a communal meal in which the bread and wine was blessed and distributed according to the hierarchy of the community. This meal was apparently considered a foreshadowing of the future messianic banquet. Members of the community gathered together and sat before the priest according their rank. The priest then blessed the firstfruits of the bread and the new wine and ate, followed by the rest of those who had gathered together (see 1QS VI 3–5).

In obedience to the Bible the Essenes pursued a strict observance of sacred time—setting aside sacred days during which they remembered God and witnessed their faithfulness to the covenant. The most important of the days of worship was the Sabbath. From several of the documents at Qumran we can reconstruct their sacred calendar of 364 days, a number divisible by seven. The Qumran community observed the Feast of the Passover, Feast of Weeks, the Day of Atonement, and Feast of Tabernacles. In addition the *Temple Scroll* mentions several firstfruits festivals not mentioned in the Bible: New Barley, New Wine, New Oil, and a Wood-Offering Festival.[14]

### Repentance and Purification

From Adam to Moses and down to the time of the Essenes, the need for repentance and purification was central to the worship of God. A short prayer from Qumran illustrates this:

> And he will bless there [the God of Israel. Answering, he will say: Blessed art Thou, God of Israel. And I stand] before Thee on the feas[t] . . . Thou hast . . . me for purity . . . and his burnt offering and he will bless. Answering he will say: Blessed art Thou, [God of Israel, who hast delivered me from al]l my sins and purified me from the impure indecency and hast atoned so that I come . . . purification and the blood of the burnt offering of Thy Goodwill and the pleasing memorial.[15]

Purification was symbolized at Qumran by ritual baths taken twice a day according to Josephus.[16] The ritual was not a mechanical one. The *Rule of the Community* tells us that the wicked "must not enter the water . . . for they cannot be cleansed unless they turn away from their wickedness" (1QS V 13–4).

### Reading and Study of the Law

The *Rule of the Community* succinctly describes the importance of the study of the word of God among the Essenes:

> When these become the Community in Israel they shall separate themselves from the session of the men of deceit in order to depart into the wilderness to prepare there the Way of the Lord (?); as it is written: "In the wilderness prepare the way of the Lord, make level in the desert a highway for our God." This (alludes to) the study of the Torah wh[ic]h he commanded through Moses to do, according to everything which has been revealed (from) time to time, and according to that which the prophets have revealed by his Holy Spirit. (1QS VIII 12–6)

> And where there are ten (members) there must not be lacking there a man who studies the Torah day and night continually, each man relieving another. The Many shall spend the third part of every night of the year in unity, reading the Book, studying judgment, and saying benedictions in unity. (1QS VI 6–8)

Study was intended to increase the understanding of the Law in order to further obedience, and this study was accompanied by prayer. These passages demonstrate the reverence the Essenes had for the word of God. Of particular interest are the various biblical commentaries called *pesharim* that were found at Qumran. The Qumran community believed that they lived in the last days, that all of the prophetic books in the Old Testament saw and prophesied of their day, and that the Teacher of Righteousness had the power to interpret these texts. The Qumran texts include pesharim on the biblical books of Hosea, Micah, Nahum, Habakkuk, and Psalms. Each of these commentaries cites a

The commentary on the book of Habakkuk was written by a Jewish sectarian to show how Habakkuk the prophet had foretold the national situation of the commentator's own day, approximately 100 B.C. (Photograph courtesy John C. Trever.)

biblical passage line by line and then interprets the imagery and prophecies in these books as they apply to the Qumran community. For example, the destruction of the Chaldeans prophesied in Habakkuk is interpreted as the destruction of the Kittim—a reference to the Romans—and the arrogant man alluded to in Habakkuk 2:5–6 is interpreted as a reference to a Wicked Priest who persecuted the Teacher of Righteousness and the community at Qumran. These commentaries show how the community at Qumran viewed themselves and their role in the last days.

## Blessing and Praising the Name of the Lord

Many texts from Qumran contain hymns of praise and thanksgiving. Some of these are clearly prayers, others are identified as hymns inasmuch as they are not specifically addressed to God and refer to him in the third person. The most remarkable of these texts is a collection of over thirty hymns found in one of the original seven scrolls. The collection is called the *Thanksgiving Hymns*, or in Hebrew, the *Hodayot*—a passage of which we will look at below.

I have the privilege of working with Professor Moshe Weinfeld of Hebrew University on a collection of six small scrolls from Cave 4. Five of these scrolls are part of *Barki Nafshi*—a single text of hymns blessing the Lord, named after the opening phrase *Bless, O My Soul*. The first several lines of one of the text read as follows:

> Bless, O my soul, the Lord,
>> for all his wonders forever,
>> and blessed be his name.
> For he has delivered the soul of the poor
>> and the humble he has not despised,
>> and he has not forgotten the distress of the helpless.
> He has opened his eyes to the helpless,
>> and the cry of the orphans he has heard,
>> and he has turned his ears to their cry.
> In the abundance of his mercy he was gracious to the needy
>> and he has opened their eyes to see his ways
>> and their ears to hear his teaching.
> And he circumcised the foreskin of their heart
>> and he delivered them because of his grace
>> and he set their feet to the way.[17]

Here God is portrayed as the champion of the poor, the humble, and the helpless. As he has opened *his* eyes to their plight and *his* ears to their cry, so has he the power to open *their* eyes to see his ways and *their* ears to hear his teaching, and most importantly he has "circumcised the foreskin of their heart" and has set their feet to "the way." Elsewhere in *Barki Nafshi* there is reference to the fact that the Lord "gave them another heart" (4Q434 1 i 10). Another passage states, "My heart thou hast commanded it and my inmost parts thou hast taught well, lest thy statutes be forgotten" (4Q436 1 i 5). The Qumran community understood that true religion can only be judged by the internal man and not just by external acts, and they sang praises to the God who had the power to change their hearts.

## Conclusion

Some of the worship at Qumran is foreign to us since it is from a culture far distant from our own in time and space. However, we as Latter-day Saints recognize in the texts from Qumran many aspects of worship that resonate with our restored truth because they are based on truths revealed anciently, many of which are still found in the Old Testament. The constant expression of humility is most impressive in the hymns from the members of this covenant community. The residents of Qumran recognized that their position as the only covenant people was an exalted calling, one that must be constantly balanced and tempered by humility. We share with the community at Qumran the heritage of the Old Testament and recognize with them the need to constantly call upon the Lord God of Israel, to be obedient to his word, to obey his law of sacrifice, to seek to become holy through repentance, participate in his ordinances, to read and study his word, and to continue to bless his name.

These remarkable lines from the *Thanksgiving Hymns* capture the feelings of covenant people from all ages and provide a moment of reflection for us, the covenant people of the latter days:

> And I, a creature [of clay
>   kneaded with water,
> a heap of dust]
>   and a heart of stone,
> for what am I reckoned to be worthy of this?
> For into an ear of dust [Thou hast put a new word]
>   and hast engraved on a heart of [stone] things everlasting.
> Thou hast caused [the straying spirit] to return
>   that it may enter into a Covenant with Thee,
> and stand [before Thee for ever]
>   in the everlasting abode,
> illumined with perfect Light for ever,
>   with [no more] darkness,
>   [for un]ending [seasons of joy]
>   and un[numbered] ages of peace.[18]

## Notes

1. Throughout the scriptures, Israel is reminded to continue to call upon the Lord, but although prayer is the very essence of worship, little instruction is given in the law of Moses specifically legislating prayer. The bulk of the legislation in Leviticus, for example, regards sacrifice. Ritual is accompanied by recitation in only a few incidents: confession upon bringing a sin offering (see Leviticus 5:5), the priest sending away the scapegoat on the Day of Atonement (see Leviticus 16:21), the recitation connected with the bringing of firstfruits (see Deuteronomy 26:1–11), and the confession of tithes (see Deuteronomy 26:12–15).

2. There are two reliable English editions of most of the Dead Sea Scroll texts. The first and most complete is Florentino García Martínez, *The Dead Sea Scrolls Translated* (Leiden: E. J. Brill, 1994). The second is Geza Vermes, *The Dead Sea Scrolls in English*, 4th ed. (London: Penguin Books, 1995), which will soon be expanded in a 5th edition.

3. See James C. VanderKam, *The Dead Sea Scrolls Today* (Grand Rapids, Mich.: Eerdmans, 1994). This is one of the best introductions to the scrolls and their study.

4. A good general survey of prayer at Qumran can be found in Lawrence H. Schiffman, *Reclaiming the Dead Sea Scrolls* (Philadelphia: Jewish Publication Society, 1994), 289–312. The first full-length comprehensive study of the prayer texts from Qumran was recently published by Bilhah Nitzan, *Qumran Prayer and Religious Poetry* (Leiden: E. J. Brill, 1994).

5. Josephus, *Jewish War* 2.8.5. These English translations of Josephus are taken from the edition of the works of Josephus, translated by H. Thackeray et al., Loeb Classical Library (1927).

6. *Rule of the Community* (1QS) X 13–6. This and subsequent translations of the *Rule of the Community* are taken from a recent edition of the text translated by Elisha Qimron and James H. Charlesworth, *Rule of the Community and Related Documents*, vol. 1 of *The Dead Sea Scrolls*, ed. James H. Charlesworth et al., (Louisville: Westminster John Knox Press, 1994).

7. See Shemaryahu Talmon, "The Emergence of Institutionalized Prayer in Israel in Light of Qumran Literature," in *The World of Qumran from Within: Collected Studies* (Leiden: E. J. Brill, 1989), 209 (pp. 200–243).

8. The history of Jewish prayer is recounted in a popular work edited by Raphael Posner, Uri Kaploun, and Shalom Cohen entitled *Jewish Liturgy: Prayer and Synagogue Service through the Ages* (Jerusalem: Keter Publishing House, 1975).

9. For example, Moshe Weinfeld has identified fragment 2 of 4Q434 as a form of *Grace after Meals for Mourners* and hymns from the *Psalms Scroll* of Cave 11 as containing elements congruent with the *Morning Benediction*. See Moshe Weinfeld, "Grace after Meals in Qumran," *Journal of Biblical Literature* 111 (1992): 427–40, and "Prayer and Liturgical Practice," in *The Dead Sea Scrolls: Forty Years of Research*, ed. Devorah Dimant and Uriel Rappaport (Leiden: E. J. Brill, 1992), 241–58.

10. See the edition of the scroll prepared by J. A. Sanders, *The Dead Sea Psalms Scroll* (Ithaca, N.Y.: Cornell University Press, 1967).

11. *Apocryphal Psalms* (11QPs[a]) XXVII, in Vermes, *Dead Sea Scrolls in English.*

12. A readable study of this intriguing document with many illustrations can be found in Yigael Yadin, *The Temple Scroll: The Hidden Law of the Dead Sea Sect* (London: Weidenfeld and Nicolson, 1985).

13. *Liturgical Prayer* (1Q34 and 1Q34bis) II, in Vermes, *Dead Sea Scrolls in English.*

14. See Yadin, *The Temple Scroll,* 84–111.

15. *Purification Ritual* (4Q512) VII, in Vermes, *Dead Sea Scrolls in English.*

16. Josephus, *Jewish War* 2.129.132.

17. *Barki Nafshi* (4Q434) 1 i 1–4. This and subsequent translations of the *Barki Nafshi* are by the author. Complete translations of this text can be found in García Martínez, *Dead Sea Scrolls Translated* and Vermes, *Dead Sea Scrolls in English.*

18. *Thanksgiving Hymns* (1QH) XVIII 25–31, in Vermes, *Dead Sea Scrolls in English.*

# CHAPTER 5

# MESSIANIC HOPES IN THE QUMRAN WRITINGS[1]

*Florentino García Martínez*

In the first twenty-five years which followed the discoveries and first publications of the texts from Qumran few topics were so widely discussed as that of "messianism."[2] The reason for this interest is easy to understand. In most of the other Jewish writings of the Second Temple period, the figure of the Messiah either does not feature or plays a very secondary role. In contrast, the new texts expressed not only the hope of an eschatological salvation but introduced into this hope the figure (or the figures) of a Messiah using the technical terminology. Thus they promised to clarify the origins of the messianic hope which occupies such a central position within Christianity. The expectations of the first years of research were not fulfilled and the reaction was not long in coming. The interest in "Qumran messianism" moved rapidly to a secondary level on the agenda of Qumran studies.[3]

*Florentino García Martínez is professor at the University of Groningen, the Netherlands, where he heads the Qumran Institute. This chapter is reprinted from* The People of the Dead Sea Scrolls, *ed. Florentino García Martínez and Julio Trebolle Barrera (Leiden: E. J. Brill, 1995).*

In publications of the last few years a new interest in the topic of Qumran messianism is evident, not dependent on the messianic idea of the New Testament but as an object of study in its own right. New studies appear regularly and abundantly.[4] It would not be necessary, though, to deal with the topic again except that, in the course of 1992, several texts were published which throw new light on Qumran messianism[5] but have not as yet been incorporated into an overall view of the problem.

My intention is simply to present the messianic texts recovered, that is, *all* the texts from the Qumran library (published or unpublished) in which are found references to the figure of the Messiah using the technical term, or to various other messianic figures, agents of eschatological salvation who are not referred to with the actual term Messiah. Naturally, I will discuss in more detail the texts which until now have been studied less and much more briefly those of which the content has been analyzed at length in the past. Unlike the presentation of other scholars,[6] I make no distinction between texts which can be considered sectarian and those whose character is more uncertain. This is because I am convinced that the simple fact of these texts being included in the sectarian library is enough to guarantee that their content was seen as in agreement with the basic thought of the group. Also these texts whose origin is difficult to determine reflect the development of biblical ideas prevalent in the period when the real sectarian texts were composed.

The picture that emerges is fragmentary and kaleidoscopic, like the texts themselves. We cannot forget that we find ourselves before an accumulation of texts produced during a period of not less than two hundred years. They can reflect perfectly well different perceptions, changes and transformations of a single idea. The library of Qumran is uniform but it is not one-dimensional or monolithic. We cannot expect more uniformity in it than is found in the Hebrew Bible, the base text which forms the foundation of all later developments.

In none of the 39 times where the Hebrew Bible uses the word "Messiah" does this word have the precise technical meaning of the title of the eschatological figure whose coming will bring in the era of salvation.[7] The "Messiahs" of the Old Testament are figures of the present, generally the king (in Isaiah 54:1 it is Cyrus) and more rarely, priests, patriarchs or prophets. And in the two cases when Daniel uses the word, they are two persons whose identity is difficult to determine, though certainly not "messianic" figures. Later tradition was certainly to re-interpret some of these Old Testament allusions to the "Messiah" as "messianic" predictions. However, the roots of the ideas which later would use the title of "Messiah" to denote the figures who would bring eschatological salvation, are found in other Old Testament texts which do not use the word "Messiah." Texts such as the blessings of Jacob (Genesis 49:10), Balaam's oracle (Numbers 24:7), Nathan's prophecy (2 Samuel 7), and the royal psalms (such as Psalm 2 and Psalm 110) would be developed by Isaiah, Jeremiah, and Ezekiel in the direction of hope in a future royal "Messiah," heir to the throne of David. The promises of the restoration of the priesthood in texts such as Jeremiah 33:14–26 (missing from the LXX) and the oracle about the high priest Joshua included in Zecariah 3, were to act as a starting point for later hope in a priestly "Messiah." Similarly, the double investiture of the "sons of oil," Zerubbabel and Joshua, in Zecariah 6:9–14 would be the starting point of the hope in a double "Messiah," reflecting a particular division of power already present since Moses and Aaron. In the same way, the presence of the triple office: king, priest, prophet, combined with the announcement of the future coming of a "prophet like Moses" of Deuteronomy 18:15,18 and with the real hope in the return of Elijah of Malachi 3:23, would act as the starting point for the development of a hope in the coming of an agent of eschatological salvation, whether called "Messiah" or not. Similarly, the presentation of the mysterious figure of the "Servant of YHWH" in chapters 40–55 of Isaiah, as an alternative to traditional messianism in the perspective of the restoration, would result in the development of a hope in a "suffering Messiah." Also, the announcement of Malachi 3:1 that God was to send his "angel" as a messenger to prepare his coming would permit the development of hope in an eschatological mediator of non-terrestrial origin.

This complex of such different "messianic" hopes, barely alluded to in the Hebrew Bible, are included and developed in the manuscripts from Qumran. The exception, perhaps, is the figure of the "Son of Man," a figure derived from Daniel 7, who reaches his full messianic development in the *Book of the Parables of Enoch*. About him, however, the manuscripts from Qumran seem to maintain a silence which does not fail to be surprising, given the influence of Daniel on the Qumran writings and the presence among them of various pseudo-Danielic compositions. All the other potentially messianic figures of the Old Testament occur in the writings from Qumran, in various stages of development. Analysis of the texts containing these references permits us to outline the complex picture of the messianic hopes of the community.

We begin with those texts which actually mention a single messianic figure, either because he was the only one hoped for or because the chances of preservation have deprived us of the passages in which other messianic figures were mentioned. We end with those texts in which several messianic figures occur together.

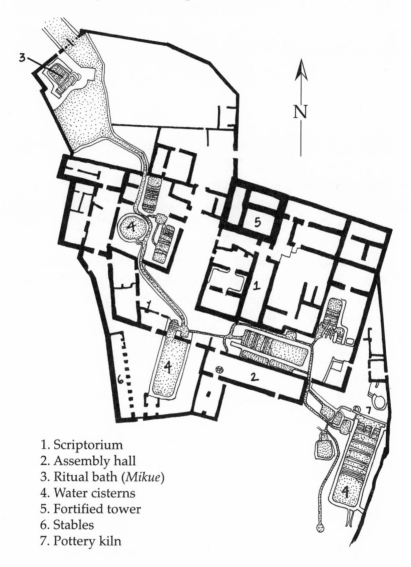

1. Scriptorium
2. Assembly hall
3. Ritual bath (*Mikue*)
4. Water cisterns
5. Fortified tower
6. Stables
7. Pottery kiln

This map illustrates several of the features of Qumran. Compare these features to those visable in the aerial view pictured on page 187, and the model pictured on page 41.

# I Texts which Mention a Single Messianic Figure

## 1 Davidic Messianism

At Qumran we find a series of texts which contain the elaboration of the basic lines of royal and davidic messianism of Old Testament origin, exactly as expressed in texts such as Jeremiah 23:5–6, Balaam's Oracle in Numbers 24:17, and Psalm 2. These texts prove to us that within the community, hope in a "Messiah-King" was very much alive. The move from allusion to an anointed-King to hope in an "Anointed One," who would come in the future as a King, is to be found in the following texts:

### 1.1  4Q252(4QpGenᵃ)

This first text shows us that within the Qumran community the famous blessing of Judah by Jacob of Genesis 49:8–12 was already interpreted in a clear messianic sense, so confirming the antiquity of the messianic interpretation of this text found in the Palestinian Targum.[8] The text in question comes from a discontinuous *pesher* on Genesis which has still not been published in full, but of which the messianic section has been known since 1956 as *4QPatriarchal Blessings*.[9] This composition is preserved in three fragmentary copies (4Q252, 253, and 254), of which 4Q252 is the longest. From what can be deduced from the fragments preserved, the work commented on selected excerpts from Genesis: the story of the flood, the curse on Canaan, the covenant with Abraham, the Sodom and Gomorrah episode, Esau's descendants and the blessings of Jacob. The commentary on these blessings, acknowledged as an independent unit,[10] filled at least three columns of the text.[11]

The literary form of the work is that of a discontinuous or thematic *pesher*. This is proved by the introductory formulas, "as it is written" (III 1), "as he said" (IV 2) or the resumptive use of pronouns (V 2,3) and by the actual use of the technical term *pesher* in IV 2. This itself shows us that it is an original composition from the Qumran community, a fact evident from the use of the expression "the men of the community" in V 5 and of the formula "as he said through Moses in respect of the last days" in IV 2. As a *pesher*, then, the text attempts to offer us the deeper meaning of the biblical text. For the community, Jacob's blessing of Judah contains the coming of the "Messiah" and actually refers to it. The text in question (4Q252 V 1–7) can be translated as follows:

> ₁ A sovereign shall [not] be removed from the tribe of Judah. While Israel has the dominion, ₂ there will [not] lack someone who sits on the throne of David. For "the staff" is the covenant of royalty, ₃ [and the thou]sands of Israel are "the feet." *Blank* Until the messiah of justice comes, the branch ₄ of David. For to him and to his descendants (to them) has been given the covenant of royalty over his people for all everlasting generations, which ₅ he has observed [. . .] the Law with the men of the community for ₆ [. . .] it is the assembly of the men of [. . .] ₇ [. . .] He gives (Florentino García Martínez, trans., *The Dead Sea Scrolls Translated,* translated into English by Wilfred G. E. Watson [Leiden: E. J. Brill, 1994], 215. All subsequent translations are also from this work, hereinafter cited as DSST.)

To the extent that the fragmentary nature of the text allows one to ascertain, each element of the biblical quotation has been supplied with its interpretation.[12] The Hebrew word *šebeṭ* has been interpreted in its double meaning of "sceptre" and "tribe." Further, sceptre has been understood as "sovereign," and while not going as far as the radical interpretation of the Palestinian Targum which translates explicitly as "king," has the same implications. "The staff" is understood as the covenant of royalty and not as the Interpreter of the Law as in CD VI 7. These expressions place the interpretation squarely in the perspective of the promise of dynastic succession, culminating, as the text states, in the coming of the "Messiah." The equation of "the feet" with the thousands of Israel highlights the military context of the promised royalty. PAM 41.708 (*FE* 409) shows the existence of a *Blank* in the manuscript, and this fact explains why the expression "Messiah of justice" is presented as equivalent to the mysterious *šiloh* of the biblical text. The expression is unique in the texts from Qumran, but the parallel with the Teacher of Righteousness makes it clear that its meaning is none other than the true, lawful Messiah.[13] The clear dependence of the expression on Jeremiah 23:5 and 33:15: "In those days I shall raise up for David a lawful shoot who will do what is right and just," also shows the polemical nature of the expression in the anti-Hasmonaean context of the community. It allows us, therefore, to set this development of a hope in a "messiah king" for the end of times within an apocalyptic context. The most logical antecedent of the clause "which he has observed" seems to be "his people," but the break in the manuscript does not permit the meaning of "his people" to be determined. The union with the men of the community in the observance of (all the precepts of) the Law leads us to suppose that from the viewpoint of the text the kingdom of the "Messiah" is limited to the loyal people. This would mean the members of the Qumran community, but such a conclusion goes beyond the preserved evidence. The loss of the rest of the text also prevents us from knowing in what sense the reference to the peoples of the Genesis text was interpreted. The reconstruction of "to whom the peoples owe obedience" in the lacuna is no more than one of the reconstructions possible. It is suggested by the resumptive pronoun, and *keneset* is only used one other time in all the texts (4QpNah III 7), in a negative sense, referring to the association of those seeking easy interpretations.

In spite of that, the general lines of the text are clear enough to assure us that in Qumran interpretation, Jacob's blessing of Judah was seen as a promise of the restoration of the davidic monarchy and of the perpetuity of his royal office. And since the future representative of the dynasty is identified not only as the shoot of David, but also explicitly as the "true anointed," there remains no doubt about the "messianic" tone of the text. Unfortunately, the details which the text provides about this "Messiah" are not many. Besides his legitimate and davidic character, his inclusion in a perpetual dynasty and the military aspect of his kingdom, the text presents his coming in connection with the Qumran community and in dispute with the Hasmonaean usurpers. Unfortunately, the fragmentary nature of the text and the ambiguity of the pronouns used do not enable us to determine whether his perpetual royalty is exercised over all the people (of Israel) or only over his own people comprising those who observed the Law within the community. Nor can we determine in which sense the other "peoples" are placed in relation to his coming.

This first text, then, only reflects the traditional idea of the "Messiah," son of David. However, it is necessary to insist on one important proviso. 4Q252, in spite of being the most complete copy preserved of the work, is an extremely fragmentary manuscript. Therefore, it cannot be excluded that other messianic figures played a role in the other missing sections of the work. This proviso is not merely a methodological constraint, but is prompted by two surprising allusions found in the other two copies of the work, even more fragmentary and still unpublished. In one of the fragments of the lower part of a column of 4Q254[14] the following lines can be read clearly: "/[...] the two sons of the oil of anointing who [...] / [...] observed the precepts of God [...] / [...] because the men of the co[mmunity...]." The reference to Zecariah 4:14 leaves no doubt at all. Also, this text, as we will see further on, seems to have played an important part in the development of the two-headed messianism which we find in the writings from Qumran. In turn, the larger fragment, 4Q253,[15] which preserves remains of two columns, includes a literal quotation of Malachi 3:17–18. This text comes just before the promise of the return of Elijah, a promise which determines the hope in the eschatological prophet of the community, whose messianic character we will indicate below. These two texts do not permit any conclusion to be drawn, but they are a precious indication of the kind of material lost from our *pesher* on Genesis, and comprise a real invitation to prudence.

We will find the same hope in a shoot of David as future Messiah-King in other clearly sectarian texts. In spite of their fragmentary nature, these texts provide some more details which allow us to sketch the outlines of this figure.

### 1.2 4Q161 (4QpIsaᵃ)

The text in question belongs to a continuous *pesher* on Isaiah, of which three columns have been preserved and it provides us with the Qumran interpretation of the classic text Isaiah 11:1–5.[16] After quoting in full the biblical text in question in lines 11–17 of column III, the text offers the Qumran interpretation:

> 18 [The interpretation of the word concerns the shoot] of David which will sprout [in the final days, since] 19 [with the breath of his lips he will execute] his enemies and God will support him with [the spirit of] courage [...] 20 [...] throne of glory, [holy] crown and hemmed vestments 21 [...] in his hand. He will rule over all the

peoples and Magog $_{22}$ [. . .] his sword will judge all the peoples. And as for what he says: "He will not $_{23}$ [judge by appearances] or give verdicts on hearsay," its interpretation: $_{24}$ [. . .] according to what they teach him, he will judge, and upon his mouth $_{25}$ [. . .] with him will go out one of the priests of renown, holding clothes in his hand (DSST, 186).

The text does not use the technical term "anointed one" but simply speaks of the "shoot of David"; however, the apposition in the text cited previously of "Messiah of justice" with the "shoot of David" guarantees us that both expressions denote the same messianic person whose coming is awaited "in the final days." Just like the blessing in Genesis 49:10, the passage Isaiah 11:1–5 is interpreted within the Qumran community as a messianic prediction. It is clear that it is a "Messiah-King," from the dynastic connotations of the term used: "shoot of David." It is also clear from the allusions to the attributes of his royalty: the throne of glory, the crown and his embroidered clothes. Our text stresses the military character of the hoped for "Messiah," described to us as a victorious warrior. The destruction of his enemies and dominion over all the peoples, including the archetypal enemy Magog, are the results of his action. He also describes to us his judicial function; but although this will be extended to all the peoples, it is subject to the instruction and authority which he will receive. The lacuna has deprived us of express mention of these instructors and guides of this "Messiah," but in view of the subordination of the "Messiah of Israel" to the priests in 1QSa II 11–21, it is most probable that it was the priests who, with their instruction and with their authority, guided the judgments of the "Messiah."

Once the messianic interpretation of Isaiah 11:1–5 is established, the application of this text to a person who recurs with frequency in the Qumran writings and who is called the "Prince of (all) the congregation"[17] allows us to understand that this person is no other than the "shoot of David" and the "Messiah of justice." Two of the texts which apply the prophecy of Isaiah to the "Prince of the congregation" are the following:

### 1.3 1Q28b (1QSb) V 20–29

20 *Blank* Of the Instructor. To bless the prince of the congregation, who [. . .] 21 [. . .] And he will renew the covenant of the Community for him, to establish the kingdom of his people for ever, [to judge the poor with justice] 22 to rebuke the humble of the earth with uprightness, to walk in perfection before him on all his paths [. . .] 23 to establish the [holy] covenant [during] the anguish of those seeking it. May the Lord raise you to an everlasting height, like a fortified tower upon the raised rampart. 24 May [you strike the peoples] with the power of your mouth. With your sceptre may you lay waste *Blank* the earth. With the breath of your lips 25 may you kill the wicked. [May he send upon you a spirit of] counsel and of everlasting fortitude, a spirit *Blank* of knowledge and of fear of God. May 26 your justice be the belt of [your loins, and loyalty] the belt of your hips. May he place upon you horns of iron and horseshoes of bronze. You will gore like a bull [. . . you will trample the peo]ples like mud of wheels. For God has established you as a sceptre. 28 Those who rule [. . . all the na]tions will serve you. He will make you strong by his holy Name. 29 He will be like a li[on . . .] the prey from you, with no-one to hunt it. Your steeds will scatter over (DSST, 433).

This lovely blessing of the "Prince of the congregation" forms part of the *Collection of blessings* included in the same manuscript that originally contained the *Rule of the Community* and the *Rule of the Congregation*.[18] The blessing collects together the echoes from a whole series of texts which play an important role in the development of later messianic ideas, such as Numbers 24:17 and Genesis 49:9–10. But there is no doubt that Isaiah 11:1–5 provides the author with most of his ideas and expressions (Isaiah 11:4 in lines 21–22

The great *Isaiah Scroll*, which is 24.5 feet long, was found in Qumran Cave 1. It was one of the first scrolls discovered in 1947 and contains the complete text of sixty-six chapters of the book of Isaiah. (Photograph by John C. Trever.)

and 24–25; Isaiah 1:2 in line 25; Isaiah 11:5 in line 26). The long introduction which precedes the blessing proper (lines 20–23) where the figure of the "Prince of the congregation" is described as the instrument chosen by God to "establish the kingdom of his people for ever" shows clearly that he is a traditional Messiah-king, although the technical term is not used. A conclusion which the very content of the blessing confirms in full: the twofold reference to the sceptre underlines its "royal" character and the references to Isaiah 11:1–5 stresses its davidic origin; his military functions are to the fore and stressed by the reference to Micah 4:13 in line 26 and all the nations end by submitting to him. These elements agree with those we have found in the preceding texts. The new contribution of this blessing consists in presenting us with the hoped for "Messiah" in function of the eschatological community. This detail appears in the actual title by which he is called, "Prince of the congregation," a title which places him in direct relationship with the community of the last times. It also appears in the first of the functions assigned to him: to renew the covenant of the community through him.

In the preserved text of 1QSb there is no explicit mention of any other messianic figure. However, this could be due to the gaps in the text, so that from this fact no conclusion can be drawn. We possess remains of a blessing clearly intended for blessing "the priests, sons of Zadok" (III 22). It is also certainly possible, as the editor suggests, that the blessing partially preserved in II 1–III 21 was destined for the High Priest of the end of days, the Messiah of Aaron or priestly Messiah.

In 1QSb, the identification of the "Prince of the congregation" as the "shoot of David" is implicit. Therefore, it could be disputed. Fortunately, this identification is explicit in the following text, a text still partly unpublished but which has received great publicity recently. It is fragment 5 of 4Q285.

The work from which this fragment comes has been preserved in two copies[19] and was known as *Berakhot Milḥamah*. It is quite possible, though, that both copies come from the lost ending to the *War Scroll*, known through copies from Cave 1 and Cave 4. The general content of the preserved fragments, the reference in both to the destruction of the *Kittim*, the mention of the archangels Gabriel and Michael and the allusions to the "Prince of the congregation,"[20] are so many indications in this direction. Whether or not the two compositions are identical, it is certain that fragment 5 of 4Q285 is of interest for our topic.

The fragment was presented by professors R. Eisenman and M. Wise in the press, in November 1991, as containing the death of the Messiah and so providing a perfect parallel to the Christian idea and to the later rabbinic concept of the Messiah, Joseph's son, who dies in an eschatological battle. A later article by G. Vermes[21] provided the first scholarly analysis of the text, to which J. D. Tabor replied later.[22] The text in question can be translated as follows:

### 1.4  4Q285 frag. 5

*1* [. . . as] the Prophet Isaiah [said] (10:34): "[The most massive of the] *2* [forest] shall be cut [with iron and Lebanon, with its magnificence,] will fall. A shoot will emerge from the stump of Jesse [. . .] *3* [. . .] the bud of David will go into battle with [. . .] *4* [. . .] and the Prince of the Congregation will kill him, the sh[oot of David . . .] *5* [. . .] and with wounds. And a priest will command [. . .] *6* [. . .] the destruction of the Kittim [. . .] (DSST, 124).

The debate evidently centres on the interpretation of line 4 and is due both to the fragmentary nature of the text and to the very ambiguity of the Hebrew expression used. The *hiphil* form used can be vocalised as a third person plural (they will kill) or as a third person singular with a suffix (he will kill him). The use of a verb in the plural in line 3 could favour understanding the verb as a plural, assuming continuity between the two. However, the lacuna and the presence in line 5 of a verb in the singular lessen the force of this argument. On the other hand, the absence of the object marker (*'et* in Hebrew) before "Prince of the congregation" clearly counsels considering "Prince of the congregation" as the subject of the verb, although this is not a decisive argument either. Ultimately, only the context can assist us

in deciding between the two grammatically possible interpretations. However, this context does not leave any doubt
at all about the meaning of the clause.

In the text from Isaiah which the author quotes exactly,
the death of the "shoot of David" is not announced. Rather, that it will be plainly he who will judge and kill the
wicked. The Qumran interpretation of this biblical text in
4Q161, which we cited above, is even more important.
There, the "Prince of the congregation" is mentioned in column II 15 and his victorious character is also stressed and
"Lebanon" and "the most massive of the forest" are interpreted as meaning the *Kittim* who are placed in his hand
(col. III 1–8). We have seen the same victorious exaltation of
the "Prince of the congregation" in 1QSb, which also uses
the text from Isaiah and it also appears in the other Qumran
allusions to that person. In the same way, the reference to
the destruction of the *Kittim* in line 6 places us clearly in the
perspective of the *War Scroll* and of the final victory over the
powers of evil. This indicates that the interpretation according to which it is the "Prince of the congregation" who kills
his foe is the one which fits best the original biblical text and
the other interpretations of this text in the Qumran writings. This best explains all the elements preserved and is
supplied with convincing parallels in other related texts.

On the other hand, the idea of the death of this "Prince
of the congregation" at the hands of his eschatological foe is
not documented in any other Qumran text dealing with the
davidic "Messiah," or in any other of the Qumran texts
mentioning the "Prince of the congregation." The allusion
to the death of the "Anointed" in Daniel 9:25–26 or the allusions to the "Suffering Servant" of Isaiah 40–45 play no role.
Accordingly, we must conclude that the death of the "Messiah" is contextually alien to the tone of our text.

This new text supplies us in a simple and tangible way with the detail that the victory of the "Messiah son of David" will include the destruction of his eschatological foe in the war of the end of times. And the definite proof that in the Qumran texts the messianic figure of the "Prince of the congregation"[23] is the same as the "shoot of David," that is, the traditional "Messiah-king."

Another text which could refer to the same messianic figure has been published recently by E. Puech.[24] It is a fascinating text although its interpretation is not without problems. The manuscript had been described by J. Starcky in 1956: "Un beau texte mentionne le Messie, mais les bienfaits du salut eschatologique, évoqués d'après Is XLss et Psalms CXLVI, sont attribués directement à Adonai" ["A lovely text mentions the Messiah, but the benefits of eschatological salvation evoked, according to Isaiah 40ff. and Psalm 146, are attributed directly to Adonai"].[25] The reference to the "Messiah" appears in the best preserved fragment, frag. 2, col. II:

### 1.5  4Q521 2 II

*1* [for the heav]ens and the earth will listen to his Messiah, *2* [and all] that is in them will not turn away from the holy precepts. *3* Be encouraged, you who are seeking the Lord in his service! *Blank 4* Will you not, perhaps, encounter the Lord in it, all those who hope in their heart? *5* For the Lord will observe the devout, and call the just by name, *6* and upon the poor he will place his spirit, and the faithful he will renew with his strength. *7* For he will honour the devout upon the throne of eternal royalty, *8* freeing prisoners, giving sight to the blind, straightening out the twisted. *9* Ever shall I cling to those who hope. In his mercy he will jud[ge,] *10* and from no-one shall the fruit [of] good [deeds] be delayed, *11* and the Lord will perform marvellous acts such as have not existed, just as he sa[id] 12 for he will heal the badly wounded and will make the dead live, he will proclaim good news to the meek 13 give lavishly [to the need]y, lead the exiled and enrich the hungry. 14 [. . .] and all [. . .] (DSST, 394).

The first problem which the text presents is that of determining whether the first line refers to one "Messiah" (as we have translated) or to several. The Hebrew text clearly reads *lemešiho*, but as the editor notes, in Qumran Hebrew the form could also be read as a plural (and in fact quite a number of scholars translate *lemešiho* of CD II 12 "his anointed ones" in the plural without correcting to *lemešihy*), which is why Pucch translates cautiously "His Messiah(s)." If I have opted conclusively for a translation in the singular, this is due to the presence of the same word in fragment 8,9, but in a form which is obviously plural[26] and seems to denote the prophets (or, according to Puech, the priests). Also because the parallel in line 6 "his spirit . . . with his strength" seems to favour clearly the interpretation of the word in the singular with the suffix clearly referring to God.

The text, then, deals here with a single "Messiah." It is not easy, though, to determine whether this person is the "Davidic Messiah" or another "messianic" figure, since the only thing the text tells us about him is that "the heavens and the earth will listen to him" and that in his era "all that is in them will not turn away from the precepts of the holy ones."[27] A fragmentary reference to his "sceptre" in the next column (frag. 2 III 6) could point us towards the "royal Messiah." However, partly the reading is uncertain and partly there is no way of proving that this person is the same as the "Messiah" of II 1.[28] The only indication I find in the text to identify this "Messiah" with the "Prince of the congregation" is that the horizon of eschatological salvation which the Lord achieves during his age seems to be limited to the eschatological congregation, the assembly of the faithful in the last times. It is certain that nearly all the formulas used are rooted in the bible, but the whole set of promises is certainly limited to those who seek the Lord, hope in him and persevere in his service. In themselves these expressions can of course refer to all the faithful of Israel. However, there is a twofold mention of the "devout" (the *hasidim* who will be rewarded with the "throne of eternal royalty") which frames the references derived from Psalm 146. And, one of the actions of this messianic age is precisely the elimination of physical obstacles which hinder belonging to the Community. These two factors seem to indicate that the horizon of the eschatological salvation which the Lord achieves in the age of his "Messiah" is limited to the members of the eschatological congregation. This could indicate that in our text the simple title "Messiah" was used as a reference to the "davidic Messiah," the "Prince of the congregation," whom the 1QSb presents in strict relationship to the congregation.

The only study of this manuscript which has appeared so far[29] considers that our text does in fact speak of the davidic "Messiah." No other argument is adduced except the assertion (clearly false) that in Qumran (with the possible exception of 1QS) only one "Messiah" was hoped for. According to the authors of this study, the person described in 4Q521 would be the direct antecedent to the Christian concept of the "Messiah." Their argument is twofold. The supposition that 4Q521 presents the "Messiah" raising the dead. And the parallel to the expressions in line 12 of Matthew 11:4–5 and Luke 7:22–23, the reply to the Baptist's embassy, in which are described the signs of the arrival of the "Messiah." This second statement is correct inasmuch as the combination in a single phrase of the resurrection of the dead with the announcement of good news to the *'anawim,* which comes from Isaiah 6:1, was not previously documented outside the New Testament. But the first supposition, which sees the "Messiah" as an agent of the portentous actions of eschatological salvation, seems completely mistaken and is simply the result of reading the manuscript incorrectly.

In line 10 they read "and [in his good]ness [for ever. His] Holy [Messiah] will not delay [in coming]," supporting their reconstruction with the use of this same expression in 1Q30. However, both the readings "and in his goodness" and "Holy" are palaeographically impossible; the strokes purported to be there do not match the traces preserved. Just as false is their reading "his work" in line 11, which besides being syntactically odd, deprives the following verbs of a subject. With the editor, read "he will do."

Wise-Tabor feel obliged to accept that the Lord is the agent of the deeds announced in lines 5–9 (among which are found some of the elements that also appear in the New Testament texts, such as the cure of the blind men), but they suppose a change of subject starting from line 10. For that they insert a mention of the "Messiah"[30] in the lacuna of line 10. And in line 11 they insert an idea which not only does not appear in the text if read correctly, it is even contrary to the thought of the whole Hebrew Bible: the idea that there are wonderful actions (in the positive sense) which are not the work of the Lord. Wise-Tabor translate the lines in question as follows: "(10) a[nd in His] go[odness forever. His] holy [Messiah] will not be slow [in coming.] (11) And as for the wonders that were not the work of the Lord, when he (i.e. the Messiah) [come]s (12) then he will heal the sick, resurrect the dead, and to the poor announce glad tidings." However all these speculations are unnecessary if the text is read correctly. In it, the Messiah does not raise up the dead, nor are there wonderful deeds which are not the work of

God. What the text teaches us is that in the final epoch, in the time of the "Messiah," God will perform wonderful deeds as he has promised and the resurrection of the dead (those who have been faithful, of course[31]) will be one of the wonderful deeds.

These texts are sufficient proof for us that the hope in a future "Messiah," heir to the davidic promises, which was to comprise the core of later rabbinic messianism, was very much present in the thought of the Qumran community. However, unlike later messianism, the messianic hopes of the community were not limited to this figure of the Messiah-King, but at the same time several of the other potentially messianic figures of the Old Testament were developed.

## 2 Priestly Messianism

Together with the King, the High Priest is one of the main individuals to receive an "anointing" in the Hebrew Bible. There is nothing unusual, then, that within the Old Testament we already find indications of the possible development of these references to the High Priest as "anointed one"—in the course of hope in a priestly agent of salvation in the eschatological era—together with the "anointed one" of royal character. It is in this sense, I think, that the vision of Zecariah 3 and its development in Zecariah 6:9–14 must be interpreted. In the first text, the future messianic age is clearly dominated by the figure of the High Priest Joshua, while the "shoot" only appears in passing and in a subordinate role. Neither of these two characters therefore is explicitly called "Messiah," but both texts are open to such an interpretation. As we will see further on, this interpretation will be developed within the Qumran community into a two-headed messianism. However, a recently published

text enables us to glimpse an independent development of
the hope in the coming of the "priestly Messiah" as an agent
of salvation at the end of times.

It is an Aramaic text, one of the copies of the *Testament of
Levi,* recently published by E. Puech,[32] which contains interesting parallels to chapter 19 of the Greek *Testament of Levi*
included in the *Testaments of the XII Patriarchs.* From what
can be deduced from the remains preserved, the protagonist of the work (probably the patriarch Levi, although it
cannot be completely excluded that it is Jacob speaking to
Levi) speaks to his descendants in a series of exhortations.
He also relates to them some of the visions which have been
revealed to him. In one of them, he tells them of the coming
of a mysterious person. Although the text is hopelessly
fragmentary it is of special interest since it seems to evoke
the figure of a "priestly Messiah." This "Messiah" is described with the features of the Suffering Servant of Isaiah,
as J. Starcky indicated in his first description of the manuscript.[33] The two longest and most important fragments of
this new text can be translated as follows:

### 2.1 4Q541 frag. 9 col. I

*1* [. . .] the sons of the generation [. . .] *2* [. . .] his wisdom.
And he will atone for all the children of his generation,
and he will be sent to all the children of *3* his people. His
word is like the word of the heavens, and his teaching,
according to the will of God. His eternal sun will shine *4*
and his fire will burn in all the ends of the earth; above
the darkness his sun will shine. Then, darkness will vanish *5* from the earth, and gloom from the globe. They will
utter many words against him, and an abundance of *6*
lies; they will fabricate fables against him, and utter every
kind of disparagement against him. His generation will
change the evil, *7* and [. . .] established in deceit and in

violence. The people will go astray in his days and they
will be bewildered (DSST, 270).

The preserved text does not actually call this person "Messiah." In spite of that, and in spite of the fragmentary condition in which the text has reached us, there is no doubt that
it is possible to recognise the person described as a messianic figure whose coming is announced in the future. That
this future is the eschatological future is evident since it is
described as the period of the kingdom of light. During it,
darkness will vanish from the globe, but a section of the
people will remain in error and directly oppose this emis-
sary. The priestly character of this figure is indicated expressly by his atoning character: "And he will atone for all
the children of his generation." This same person will
clearly have to teach and will possess supreme wisdom
since "His word is like the word of the heavens."

The agreement of the person thus described with the
"Messiah-priest" described in chapter 18 of the Greek *Testament of Levi* is surprising.[34] At least it shows us that the presence of this priestly figure in the *Testaments of the XII Patriarchs* should not simply be ascribed to interpolations or
Christian influence. Rather, it is a development which exists
already within Judaism. This text also shows us that the
portrayal of this "Messiah-priest" with the features of the
"Suffering Servant" of Deutero-Isaiah is not an innovation
of purely Christian origin either, but the result of previous
developments. Our text stresses that although he would be
sent "to all the sons of his people," the opposition to this
figure, "light of the nations" (Isaiah 42:6) would be great:
"They will utter many words against him, and an abundance of lies; they will fabricate fables against him, and
utter every kind of disparagement against him" (compare
Isaiah 50:6–8; 53:2–10). What is more, according to the

editor, it cannot be excluded that the Aramaic text even contained the idea of the violent death of this "Messiah-priest." In other words, this opposition would reach its ultimate outcome as in Isaiah 53. His argument comes from the other fairly extensive fragment of the work, in which possible allusions to a violent death by crucifixion are found. However, to me this interpretation seems problematic. The fragment in question can be translated as follows:

### 2.2 4Q541 frag. 24 col. II

₂ Do not mourn for him [. . .] and do not [. . .] ₃ And God will notice the failings [. . .] the uncovered failings [. . .] ₄ Examine, ask and know what the dove has asked; do not punish one weakened because of exhaustion and from being uncertain a[ll . . .] ₅ do not bring the nail near him. And you will establish for your father a name of joy, and for your brothers you will make a tested foundation rise. ₆ You will see it and rejoice in eternal light. And you will not be of the enemy. *Blank* ₇ *Blank* (DSST, 270).

The first lines are very confused and lines 4 and 5 present problems both of reading and of interpretation. The reading we have translated as "being uncertain" and the editor as "being hanged" is not certain and the interpretation of the previously unknown Aramaic word, which we translate "nail," is not definite. In addition, it seems impossible to prove that both fragments refer to the same person. What really is clear is that both fragments are composed in a distinctive style and that the second is direct address. Its admonishing character, the formula used, and the fact that the *Blank* of line 6 is followed by a completely blank line suggests that this fragment has actually preserved the end of the work, or at least, the end of a large section. The exhortation not to mourn could be understood perfectly before the imminent death of the Patriarch, just as the final promise could refer to his descendant. Whatever might be the possible allusion to the death of the expected "Messiah-priest," the identification of this figure with the "Servant" of Isaiah seems confirmed by the parallels indicated in fragment 9. In any case, the idea that the eventual death of the "Messiah-priest" could have an atoning role, as Christian tradition attributes to the death of the "Servant," is excluded from our text since the atonement he achieves (frag. 9 II 2) remains in the perspective of the cult.

As far as I know, this is the only text which in the preserved sections deals with the priestly "Messiah" alone. However, many other texts refer to this figure when speaking of a two-fold messianism. This is the two-headed messianism in which we are presented with the "davidic or royal Messiah" and the "levitical or priestly Messiah" together. They are called the "Messiahs of Israel and of Aaron" respectively. Before going on to consider compositions which mention several "Messiahs," however, we must present another text which refers to another type of "messianic" figure, a superhuman agent of eschatological salvation.

### 3 A Heavenly "Messiah"

The title of this paragraph could cause surprise and even seem contradictory. It is perfectly understandable that hope in a superhuman agent of eschatological salvation could have developed in the Judaism of the period. To consider this agent of eschatological salvation as a "Messiah" could appear to be not just an unacceptable broadening of the concept of "Messiah" but even a broadening which empties the concept of "Messiah" of its deepest characteristic, its human dimension. It is difficult enough to imagine the possibility of a superhuman person being considered as "anointed" (angels certainly did not receive an anointing). Even more, the human nature of the "Messiahs" which we have seen so far, should be strongly stressed both in the davidic descendance of the "Messiah-king" and in the cultic perspective in which the "Messiah-priest" performs his atonement. If, in addition, it is accepted that the technical term "anointed" does not occur in the text in question, the attempt to consider it as "messianic" could seem to be somewhat artificial, and the semantic widening of the term "Messiah" so implied as meaningless.

And yet it seems difficult to avoid using the adjective "messianic" to characterise the hero of this text, since the functions attributed to him really are "messianic" functions. Other Jewish writings, not from Qumran, describing a superhuman agent of eschatological salvation, use the technical term "Messiah" as one of the names for the saving figure which they describe. This proves that the widening of the semantic field of "Messiah" had already taken place in the Judaism of the period and forces us not to exclude these texts *a priori*, under pain of ignoring one of the possible developments of "messianic" hope reflected in the manuscripts preserved. The texts I am referring to are, of course, *The Parables of Enoch* and *IV Esdras*. The first occasionally uses the term "Messiah" (in 48:10 and 52:4) together with the more common titles of "Chosen One" and above all "Son of Man"[35] to denote an existing, transcendental figure of celestial origin. In the vision included in chapter 13 by the author of *IV Esdras*, a person "like a man," called "Messiah" in 7:28 and 12:32 and more often "son/ servant of God," is clearly presented also as an existing, transcendental person of celestial origin.[36] Both figures are called "Messiah" in these texts, in spite of their superhuman nature and in spite of being described with images traditionally associated with the divinity. Accordingly, as

Collins correctly observes,[37] "the understanding of 'messiah' is thereby qualified." These parallels in two compositions, of which the Jewish origin does not seem to be doubted, justifies our inclusion of the following text in our study.

A few lines of this text have been known for quite some time[38] and have been extensively studied.[39] However, the recent complete publication of the fragment[40] which informs us of the last five lines of column II allows a fuller analysis. It is the only fragment preserved of an Aramaic composition dated palaeographically to the first half of the 1st century. This fragment comes from the end of a leather leaf and preserves traces of sewing to the following sheet; in it is preserved a complete column of nine lines and approximately half of the preceding column. The text can be translated as follows:

4Q246 col. 1

> $_1$ [. . .] settled upon him and he fell before the throne $_2$ [. . .] eternal king. You are angry and your years $_3$ [. . .] they will see you, and all shall come for ever. $_4$ [. . .] great, oppression will come upon the earth $_5$ [. . .] and great slaughter in the city $_6$ [. . .] king of Assyria and of Egypt $_7$ [. . .] and he will be great over the earth $_8$ [. . .] they will do, and all will serve $_9$ [. . .] great will he be called and he will be designated by his name (DSST, 138).

Col. II

> $_1$ He will be called son of God, and they will call him son of the Most High. Like the sparks $_2$ of a vision, so will their kingdom be; they will rule several years over $_3$ the earth and crush everything; a people will crush another people, and a city another city. $_4$ *Blank* Until the people of God arises and makes everyone rest from the sword. $_5$

> His kingdom will be an eternal kingdom, and all his
> paths in truth and uprigh[tness]. ₆ The earth (will be) in
> truth and all will make peace. The sword will cease in the
> earth, ₇ and all the cities will pay him homage. He is a
> great God among the gods (?). ₈ He will make war with
> him; he will place the peoples in his hand and cast away
> everyone before him. ₉ His kingdom will be an eternal
> kingdom, and all the abysses (DSST, 138).

I described the contents of the text as known in 1983:

> The text tells us that someone (a seer?) falls down in front
> of a king's throne and addresses him. He describes to him
> the evils to come, among which reference to Assyria and
> Egypt play an important role. Even more important will
> be the apparition of a mysterious person to whom will be
> given the titles of "son of God" and "son of the Most
> High," a person who "will be great upon the earth" and
> whom "all will serve." His appearance will be followed
> by tribulations, but these will be as fleeting as a spark
> and will only last "until the people of God arises." The
> outcome will be the end of war, an eternal kingdom in
> which all will make peace, cities will be conquered, be-
> cause the great God will be with him (with his people?)
> and he will make all his enemies subject to him.[41]

First I set out the interpretations of Milik (who identified
the mysterious person as Alexander Balas), Fitzmyer (who
applied the titles to a royal but nonmessianic person, heir to
David's throne) and Flusser (who saw a reference to Antichrist in this mysterious person) and the reasons why they
seemed insufficient. I then proposed understanding the
person to which the text refers as an "Eschatological liberator" of angelic, that is to say, non-human nature, a figure
similar in functions to those which 11QMelch ascribes to
Melchizedek or 1QM to the "Prince of Light" or to the arch-
angel Michael. E. Puech, the editor of the whole text, thinks

that the preserved text does not allow definitive resolution between an "historicizing" interpretation like Milik's and a "messianic" interpretation, towards which his preferences seem inclined. Puech seems to exclude my interpretation for two reasons. It is not certain that 4Q246 is a composition of Qumran origin and because, in his opinion, "the 'heavenly' figures who are the mediators of salvation in ancient Judaism, Enoch, Elijah, Melkizedek or the Son of God have not, strictly speaking, received the title of 'messiah.' "[42] However, as we have indicated, this statement is not completely correct. Also, the parallels I noted with ideas contained in other Qumran writings, may not be determinative in assigning a sectarian origin to the composition, but do at least make it completely compatible with the thought of the Qumran group.

Professor Florentino García Martínez and his wife, Annie, in their home in Groningen, the Netherlands. García Martínez is a world-renowned Dead Sea Scrolls scholar.

I remain convinced, then, that my interpretation of the first fragmentary column and of the first four lines of column II continues to be the best to explain the elements preserved. My description of the person in question as "angelic" was based on the parallel with other non-human figures of the Qumran texts. Perhaps it would be more correct to denote this superhuman figure simply as "heavenly." And the new lines now available confirm and emphasise this conclusion, since they describe this figure with the features of Daniel's "Son of Man."[43] The quotations from Daniel 7 are especially striking. "His kingdom will be an eternal kingdom" of column II 5 comes from Daniel 7:27 where it is applied to the "people of the holy ones of the Most High." "His kingdom will be an eternal kingdom" of column II 9 comes from Daniel 7:14, where it is applied to the "Son of Man." In the biblical text, the parallelism of both expressions in the vision and in its explanation could favour the interpretation of the "Son of Man" as a collective figure. The author of our composition, however, seems to attribute both expressions to the mysterious protagonist of the narrative, whom he considers without any doubt whatever as an individual, so anticipating the clear interpretation as an individual we find in the *Book of Parables*.

The preserved text does not completely exclude the possibility that the third person pronominal suffixes it uses, beginning with column II 5, could refer to the people of God. In fact, biblical equivalents could be found for most of the expressions used, which refer sometimes to an individual person and sometimes to a person representing the people, or to the people. In spite of this ambiguity, though, the lines published recently incline me to modify the position I had adopted in 1983, attributing these pronouns to the "people of God." I now adopt Puech's interpretation who refers them clearly to the protagonist mentioned at the end of column I and at the beginning of column II.

Puech notes that "may he raise" ["qu'il relève"] can be read in column II 4 instead of "may (the people of God) rise" ["que se (re)lève le peuple de Dieu"], and "may he make all rest" ["qu'il fasse tout reposer"] instead of "all will rest" ["tout reposera"]. This enables line 4 to be understood as the climax of the period of crisis described beforehand, enables the lofty titles given to the protagonist to be understood, since the task he has to fulfil is to bring in the situation of eschatological peace, and it enables the particle used to be given its value of a limit.[44] This interpretation is strengthened by the use of "he will judge" in column II 5, and by the statement of the cosmic dimension of his kingdom in column II 9.

This reading of the text is strengthened by the way in which the sentence in question is set out in the manuscript. The *Blank* which comes before mention of the "people of God" seems intended to emphasise that this situation of eschatological peace is precisely the conclusion of the situation described previously and is due to the activity of the protagonist, to whom the lofty titles "son of God" and "son of the Most High" are given. The *Blank* which follows this expression on the same line removes the need to make a whole series of suffixes in the following lines refer to the nearest antecedent ("the people of God," the object of the preceding phrase). They can refer to the subject of the phrase, the "son of God" and "son of the Most High."

Understood in this way, 4Q246 describes an eschatological liberator, a heavenly being similar to the "Son of Man" of Daniel 7, called "son of God" and "son of the Most High." He will be the agent to bring eschatological salvation, judge all the earth, conquer all the kings through God's power and rule over the whole universe.

This messianic interpretation of the "eschatological liberator" of 4Q246 which I proposed in 1983 agrees completely with the "messianic" interpretation proposed by Puech as an alternative to Milik's "historicising" interpretation (which he accepts as equally valid). Although Puech insists on the royal character and on the Davidic lineage of this person he ends by considering this "Messiah" as a special divinised "Messiah," similar to the Melchizedek of 11QMelch and the heavenly Son of Man.[45] And this is precisely the element which has to be emphasised here. In Qumran together with a "Messiah-king" and a "Messiah-priest" the coming of an agent of eschatological salvation was expected (who is not explicitly referred to as "Messiah" in the text) as exalted as the pre-existent "Son of Man" of the *Parables of Enoch* or like the "Messiah" of *IV Esdras*.

This same type of saviour figure of superhuman nature is found in another text (11QMelch), where the title "Messiah of the Spirit" has been partially preserved. However, this title seems to refer to the "messianic" figure of the eschatological prophet, mentioned together with the eschatological deliverer of heavenly nature who is Melchizedek. Therefore, this text must be considered among those which tell us of several messianic figures. We will discuss it briefly in what follows.

## II Texts which Mention Several Messianic Figures

### 1 Two "Messiahs": the "Messiahs of Aaron and Israel"

Perhaps the most studied and best known element of Qumran messianism is its two-headed messianism: the hope in a double "Messiah," "the Messiah of Aaron" and the "Messiah of Israel." The key text comes from the *Rule of the Community.*[46]

### 1.1 1QS IX 9–11

9 They should not depart from any counsel of the law in order to walk 10 in complete stubbornness of their heart, but instead shall be ruled by the first directives which the men of the Community began to be taught 11 until the prophet comes, and the Messiahs of Aaron and Israel. *Blank* (DSST, 13–14).

The text is crystal clear and expresses without any doubt the hope, within the Qumran community, in the future coming of the two "anointed ones" (in the plural). The "Messiah of Aaron" and the "Messiah of Israel," two figures who apparently correspond to the "priestly Messiah" and the "royal Messiah" whom we came across as separate figures in the preceding texts. Together with them, and distinct from both "Messiahs," there was hope in the eschatological future for the coming of another person: a prophet. The only thing the text tells us about these three figures is the hope in their coming. It tells us nothing about their functions, about the biblical basis which allowed their hope to develop, their possible identification with other titles used in the texts to give these figures a name. The exception is the priestly character implied in the provenance "from Aaron" of one of them and of the non-priestly character of the other who comes "from Israel." In spite of its laconic nature, this text is fundamental since it allows us to clarify a whole series of expressions which mention the "anointed one" (in the singular) of Aaron and of Israel as referring not to a single "Messiah," priest and king at the same time, but to two "Messiahs": a "Messiah-priest" and a "lay-Messiah."

There has been much discussion about the origin of this hope in a double "Messiah," who also appears in the *Testa-*

*ments of the XII Patriarchs*,[47] especially after it was known that in the oldest copy of the *Rule of the Community* (4QS[e]) the passage in question does not occur.[48] In that manuscript, the text goes straight from VIII 15 to IX 12.[49] It is impossible, though, to know whether it is an accidental omission by the copyist of something that was there in the original work, or of a later addition inserted into the copy from Cave 1. In any case, the presence of this passage in the manuscript of 1QS is enough for our purpose. It proves that this hope in a double "Messiah" existed at Qumran and guarantees that the same hope is found reflected in the other texts which they use to express it less clearly.

The text does not allow us to determine whether the first figure it introduces—a prophet—does or does not have "messianic" features. Its contrast to the "Messiahs" seems rather to indicate the opposite. But other texts which we will see later enable us to determine that this expected prophet was also considered a "messianic" figure. Of the "messianic" nature of the "Messiahs of Aaron and Israel" there can be absolutely no doubt. This messianic character is even more obvious in the other texts in the *Damascus Document*[50] which mention these two figures, although in none of these references is the word "Messiah" used in the plural.

## 1.2 CD

₂₂ *Blank* And this is the rule of the assembly ₂₃ [of the ca]mps. Those who walk in them, in the time of wickedness until there arises the messiah of Aaron ₁ and Israel, they shall be ten in number as a minimum to (form) thousands, hundreds, fifties ₂ and tens (CD XII 22–XIII 2; DSST, 43).

*Blank* And this is the exact interpretation of the regulations by which [they shall be ruled] ₁₉ [until there arises the

messiah] of Aaron and Israel.[51] He shall atone for their
sins [. . . pardon, and guilt] (CD XIV 18–19; DSST, 44).

These shall escape in the age of the visitation; but those
that remain shall be delivered up to the sword when
there comes the messiah $_{11}$ of Aaron and Israel (CD XIX
10–11; DSST, 45).

And thus, all the men who entered the new $_{34}$ covenant in
the land of Damascus and turned and betrayed and departed from the well of living waters, $_{35}$ shall not be
counted in the assembly of the people and shall not be
inscribed in their [lis]ts, from the day of the session $_1$ of
the unique Teacher until there arises the messiah of
Aaron and Israel. *Blank* (CD XIX 33– XX 1; DSST, 46).

As we have indicated, these four texts use one somewhat
ambiguous expression: "Messiah of Aaron and Israel" in
CD XII 23,[52] XIV 19 and XIX 10, and "Messiah of Aaron and
of Israel" in CD XX 1, an expression which can be translated
both by "Messiah of Aaron and of Israel" and by "Messiah
of Aaron and (Messiah) of Israel." Although the second expression can be interpreted more easily as referring to two
different persons,[53] the possibility of interpreting both
phrases as referring to a single person who comes from
Aaron and Israel at the same time, is not only an actual possibility but it is also strengthened by the fact that in CD IX
19 the expression is followed by a verb in the singular. Accordingly, several scholars have made the "Messiah" the
subject of the verb. And since the act is one of atonement,
they have concluded that the figure indicated will be that of
the "priestly Messiah" who will atone for the sins of the
people.[54] But the text already cited, 1QS IX 11, resolves the
ambiguity of the Hebrew expression. It proves that in all
these cases the most likely interpretation is one which sees
in these phrases a reference to the two "Messiahs" expected
by the community.[55]

In these four texts, the coming of these persons is expected for the "time of wickedness" and "the age of the visitation," two expressions which leave no doubt at all about the eschatological perspective in which the hope in their arrival is placed. The texts tell us hardly anything directly about the functions of these persons. The first and fourth references place his coming in relation to the structure and organization of the community in the eschatological period. The second reference relates it to the exact interpretation of the regulations; the third, to the different fates, salvation or damnation, which will befall the faithful or the unfaithful when they come. Finally, the fourth reference suggests that their coming is expected (shortly) after the disappearance of the "Unique Teacher," the historical figure we know as the "Teacher of Righteousness," and already a figure of the past at the time when this version of the *Damascus Document* was edited.

We can deduce more details about his functions from two texts from another of the manuscripts which seem to mention both figures together, the *Rule of the Congregation*.[56]

### 1.3 1QSa

11 This is the assembly of famous men, [those summoned to] the gathering of the community council, when [God] begets 12 the Messiah with them. [The] chief [priest] of the all the congregation of Israel shall enter, and all 13 [his brothers, the sons] of Aaron, the priests [summoned] to the assembly, the famous men, and they shall sit 14 befo[re him, each one] according to his dignity. After, [the Me]ssiah of Israel shall ent[er] and before him shall sit the chiefs 15 [of the clans of Israel, each] one according to his dignity, according to their [positions] in their camps and in their marches (1QSa II 11–14; DSST, 127).

17 And [when] they gather at the table of community [or

to drink] the new wine, and the table of $_{18}$ community is prepared [and] the new wine [is mixed] for drinking, [no-one should stretch out] his hand to the first-fruit of the bread $_{19}$ and of the [new wine] before the priest, for [he is the one who bl]esses the first-fruit of bread 20 and of the new wine [and stretches out] his hand towards the bread before them. Afterwards, the Messiah of Israel shall stretch out his hand $_{21}$ towards the bread. [And after, he shall] bless all the congregation of the community, each [one according to] his dignity. And in accordance with this regulation they shall act $_{22}$ at each me[al, when] at least ten m[en are gat]hered. *Blank* (1QSa II 17–22; DSST, 127–128).

These two fragments mention a "priest" and the "Messiah of Israel" as two clearly distinct figures. About the "Messiah" it apparently tells us that God "begets" him with them. The syntax is strange and the reading uncertain; but the editor is reliable in as much as either "will beget" or "will cause to be born" can be read in the manuscript.[57] This means that our text must include the ideas of Psalm 2:7, applying them to the "divine" origin of the "Messiah." Due to a lacuna, it is not possible to know for certain whether it is a question of the "anointed [priest]" (as Kuhn proposes, identifying him with the Messiah of Aaron) or of an absolute use of the "Messiah" which could instead correspond to the person which the following text denotes as "Messiah of Israel." The uncertainties of the text prevent us from attaching great weight to this person about whom the opinions of scholars are so divided.

Fortunately, there is more agreement about the identity of the priest in question. Most of the researchers recognise in him the "High Priest" of the eschatological period, whom they identify with the "Messiah of Aaron." The eschatological period is involved, as shown by the text itself, indicating that they are regulations "for the end of times" (col. I 1). The "priest" is the High Priest, as is also evident in the text which defines him as "chief of the whole congregation of Israel." This High Priest of the eschatological period is the same figure we met in the preceding texts, called "Messiah of Aaron." That is a logical deduction based on his superiority over the "Messiah of Israel" who is mentioned next, a superiority already indicated in the very formula in which they both appear together: "Messiah of Aaron and of Israel."[58] Our text emphasises the connection of this messianic figure with the congregation. It also emphasises his superior function both in relation to the other sons of Aaron, the priests, and especially the non-priestly members of the community, including the "Messiah of Israel." Both in the assemblies and in the banquet it is he who presides and occupies the most eminent position. Concerning the "Messiah of Israel" these texts emphasise his subordinate position to the priest and his military character, indicated in the terminology used which depends on Numbers and agrees with 1QM.

Another possible allusion to the functions of both "Messiahs" could be provided by 4Q375 and 4Q376, although the meaning of these two texts is ambiguous and problematic, and their interpretation is very uncertain.

Both manuscripts were published by J. Strugnell,[59] who considers them to be two possible copies of a single composition. 4Q376 is certainly another copy of the work known from several fragments from Cave 1 (1Q29), and it seems reasonable to consider these three manuscripts as copies of the same composition. In addition, the editor presents certain arguments from style in favour of identifying the composition represented in these three texts with the Moses apocryphon known as *Words of Moses* (1Q22) which would provide the narrative framework of the composition. However, this seems too problematic and in any case is not important for our purpose. What could really be important is the reference in 4Q375 1 I 9 to "the anointed priest upon whose head the oil of anointing has been poured." Similarly, the mention in 4Q376 1 III 1 of "the Prince who is over the whole congregation" in a clear military context, and in connection with "the anointed priest" mentioned in the first column of this manuscript (4Q376 1 I 1).

If 4Q375 and 4Q376 really were two copies of the same composition; if the "Prince of the whole congregation" had the same meaning in this work as in *all* the other Qumran texts where the expression is used and where it *always* denotes the "davidic Messiah"; and if it could be shown that this person is located in an eschatological context, these fragments would be very interesting for this study on messianic ideas. This would allow an allusion both to the High Priest and to the "priestly Messiah" to be seen in the "anointed priest upon whose head the oil of anointing has been poured." And in the "Prophet" an allusion to the eschatological Prophet. Further, the complex procedure by which the High Priest determines whether the prophet is true or false by means of a sacrificial rite, the investigation of hidden precepts and the oracular use of the *Urim* could be interpreted as a process of verifying whether in fact the prophet is the eschatological Prophet or not and not merely whether the prophet is true or false.

However to me it seems impossible to prove definitively the conditions upon which this interpretation rests.[60] There is no clear indication that both texts are located in an eschatological perspective. The texts can be explained perfectly as an apocryphon in which in pure deuteronomistic language the High Priest judges a false prophet who has the backing of a whole tribe which considers him as a trustworthy prophet. The process used is different from what is prescribed in Deuteronomy 13 and 18, comprising an atonement ceremony, the investigation of the divine precepts which have been hidden from the people and the oracular use of the *Urim*. And "the Prince of the whole congregation" could only be a modification of the plural form "princes of the congregation" of Exodus 16:22, Numbers 4:34, 16:2, 31:33, 32:2 and Joshua 9:15,18. Accordingly, for the moment this fascinating text must remain outside the discussion of "messianism."

### 2 Two "Messiahs": the "Prince of the Congregation" and the "Interpreter of the Law"

Together with texts which mention the two "Messiahs" of Aaron and of Israel we find others which also mention two messianic figures called by other names. We must try and establish their identity.

#### 2.1  CD VII 18–21[61]

18 . . . *Blank* And the star is the Interpreter of the law 19 who will come to Damascus as is written: (Numbers 24:13) "A star moves out of Jacob, and a sceptre arises 20 out of Israel." The sceptre is the prince of the whole congregation and when he rises he will destroy 21 all the sons of Seth. *Blank* (DSST, 38).

The "Prince of the whole congregation" is familiar to us and apart from 4Q376, where his character cannot be determined, always denotes a "messianic" figure. As in the previous texts, here he is equated with the sceptre. There is no doubt, therefore, about his identity with the "Messiah-king," the davidic "Messiah" of Jewish tradition and the "Messiah of Israel" of the other texts where the davidic character of such titles is muted. This text only tells us about the one who "will destroy all the sons of Seth,"

using the expression of Numbers 24:17, but without speci-
fying its meaning (which in the original biblical text is not
very clear either). But who is the "Interpreter of the Law"
who here appears in parallel with him? Is he a figure from
the past or from the future?

The ambiguity of the text is well known and, ultimately,
everything depends on the value of past or future given to
the participle used. The authors who are convinced that in
this *Amos-Numbers Midrash* only one messianic figure is
spoken about[62] consider the "Interpreter of the Law" as a
figure from the past. Whereas, those who see in our text an
allusion to two "messianic" figures see a figure of the future
in this same "Interpreter of the Law," contemporary with
the "Prince of the whole congregation."[63]

The strict parallelism between the two figures, the fact
that both are interpreted starting from the same biblical text
(to which later tradition was to give a clear messianic value)
and, above all, the details which 4Q174 give us about this
"Interpreter of the Law" who will come in the final times
together with the "shoot of David," a figure whom 4Q174
explicitly identifies with the "Prince of the congregation,"
are enough, in my opinion, to resolve the ambiguity of the
text in favour of the interpretation which sees reflected here
hope in two messianic figures.

It seems more difficult to determine who this "Interpreter of the Laws" is. Two interpretations have been suggested. Starcky[64] identified him with the expected
eschatological prophet although this identification starts
from a false premise, the non-separation of the two "Messiahs" of Aaron and of Israel in CD. The more prevalent opinion, following van der Woude,[65] identifies this "Interpreter
of the Law" with the "Messiah of Aaron." I.e., the
"priest-Messiah" who should be identified with the eschatological figure of Elijah. Van der Woude's reasoning

essentially is as follows. The "Interpreter of the Law" of the passage is a person from the future and thus distinct from the "Interpreter of the Law" who occurs in CD VI 7 and is a person from the past. This person is found in parallel with the "Prince of the whole congregation," who is a messianic figure identical with the "Messiah of Israel," so that he must also be a messianic figure. The title given him, "Interpreter of the Law," is very general and can denote various figures, but the specification "who will come to Damascus" (meaning Qumran) is more significant. The clause comes from 1 Kings 19:15, where Elijah receives from God the order to go to Damascus to anoint the king of Syria, the king of Israel, and the prophet Elisha. In later tradition (attested in Justin, *Dialog.* 49[66] and in the Karaite material collected by N. Wieder[67]) Elijah is portrayed as the eschatological High Priest who performs the anointing of the Messiah. In rabbinic tradition, Elijah is also portrayed as one who will resolve the halakhic problems the rabbis are unable to solve, when he returns at the end of times as a forerunner of the "Messiah." This permits van der Woude to conclude that the "Interpreter of the Law" denotes Elijah whose coming is expected at the end of times. This figure is seen as a "priestly Messiah" and thus is identical with the "Messiah of Aaron" of the other Qumran texts.

My problem with this reasoning is that the two texts which mention the eschatological figure of the "Interpreter of the Law" tell us absolutely nothing about his priestly character; the features of "prophet" seem more characteristic of Elijah than those of "priest." Accordingly, for very different reasons from those of Starcky, I feel more inclined to identify this messianic figure of the eschatological "Interpreter of the Law" with the messianic figure about whom we have not yet spoken. He is the "Prophet" expected at the end of times, whose identification with Elijah *redivivus* can be accepted without problems. The reasons for this inclination will be set out when dealing in more detail with this figure of the "eschatological Prophet."

## 2.2  4Q174 *(4QFlorilegium)*

The other text which mentions these same two "messianic" figures is known as *Florilegium*.[68]

> 10 And "YHWH de[clares] to you that he will build you a house. I will raise up your seed after you and establish the throne of his kingdom 11 [for ev]er. I will be a father to him and he will be a son to me." This (refers to the) "branch of David," who will arise with the Interpreter of the law who 12 [will rise up] in Zi[on in] the last days, as it is written: "I will raise up the hut of David which has fallen," This (refers to) "the hut of 13 David which has fallen," who will arise to save Israel. Blank (DSST, 136).

This text refers to the "Interpreter of the Law" by name. Together with him it speaks about the "branch of David," a familiar expression to denote the "Messiah-king," named "Prince of the whole congregation" in the preceding text. His identity with the "Messiah of Israel" presents no problem. Apart from their future coming, it tells us nothing about both figures. The requirement that this coming would take place in "the last days" remains important since it stresses his clear eschatological character.

## 3 Two "Messiahs": the "Heavenly Messiah" and the "Eschatological Prophet"

Another of the Qumran fragments in which the figure of a heavenly "Messiah" appears is a midrash of eschatological content, in which a heavenly person, an *elohim*, called Melchizedek, is the divine instrument of salvation and executes justice. The central part of the fragment (col. II 6–19) can be translated as follows:[69]

*6* He (Melchizedek) will proclaim liberty for them, to free them from [the debt] of all their iniquities. And this will [happen] *7* in the first week of the jubilee which follows the ni[ne] jubilees. And the day [of atonem]ent is the end of the tenth jubilee *8* in which atonement will be made for all the sons of [God] and for the men of the lot of Melchizedek. [And on the heights] he will decla[re in their] favour according to their lots; for *9* it is the time of the "year of grace" for Melchizedek, to exa[lt in the tri]al the holy ones of God through the rule of judgment, as is written *10* about him in the songs of David, who said: "Elohim will stand up in the assem[bly of God,] in the midst of the gods he judges." And about him he said: "Above it *11* return to the heights, God will judge the peoples." As for what he sa[id: "How long will yo]u judge unjustly and show partiality to the wicked? *Selah.*" *12* Its interpretation concerns Belial and the spirits of his lot, who were rebels [all of them] turning aside from the commandments of God [to commit evil.] *13* But, Melchizedek will carry out the vengeance of God's judges [on this day, and they shall be freed from the hands] of Belial and from the hands of all the sp[irits of his lot.] *14* To his aid (shall come) all "the gods of [justice"; he] is the [one who will prevail on this day over] all the sons of God, and he will pre[side over] this [assembly.] *15* This is the day of [peace about which God] spoke [of old through the words of Isa]iah the prophet, who said: "How beautiful *16* upon the mountains are the feet of the messenger who announces peace, of the mess[enger of good who announces salvation,] saying to Zion: "Your God [reigns.' "] *17* Its interpretation: The mountains are the pro[phets . . .] *18* And the messenger is [the ano]inted of the spirit about whom Dan[iel] spoke [. . . and the messenger of] ₁₉ good who announces salv[ation is the one about whom it is written that [. . .] (DSST, 139–140).

In spite of the uncertainty of the reconstructions, the broad lines of the content seem clear enough and are well known. Here, therefore, we only need to note the details which they give concerning the messianic figures to whom the text refers. The weave of the text is formed by Leviticus 25:8–13 concerning the jubilee year, Deuteronomy 15 concerning the year of release and Isaiah 61. The author also applies to Melchizedek, the protagonist, other texts from Isaiah, the Psalms and Daniel, the interpretation of which allows him to develop his ideas. The eschatological content is evident through the execution of justice and the deliverance from Belial. It is also evident because the whole is set specifically in the first week of the tenth jubilee, the final jubilee in his chronological system. In this context, the author ascribes three fundamental functions to this exalted figure: to be an avenging judge (with reference to Psalms 82:1–2 and 7:1); to be a heavenly priest who carries out atonement for his inheritance on the "day of atonement"; and to be the ultimate saviour of "the men of his lot" who destroys the kingdom of Belial and restores peace.

With the restoration of the day of peace, the text seems to introduce a new person, identified as "the messenger" of Isaiah 52:7, a text which the author combines with Isaiah 61:2–3. It defines this person as "the anointed by the spirit," clearly in the singular. Unfortunately, neither the text of Daniel nor further details have been preserved. All that we can assert about him, therefore, is that the text clearly distinguishes him from the prophets of the past, and seems to consider him as introducing the action of the "heavenly Messiah." His identification as the "eschatological Prophet," which we will study next, cannot be considered as completely proved, but is certainly the most probable.[70]

## 4 Three "Messiahs": the Eschatological Prophet

In commenting on the key text 1QS IX 11, we left in suspense the third figure who appeared there together with the "Messiahs of Aaron and of Israel" and is simply called "the Prophet": "until the prophet comes and the Messiahs of Aaron and Israel." It is obvious from his juxtaposition to the two "Messiah" figures that this person is an eschatological person. It is less evident that he is a true "messianic" figure, since unlike the other two he is not termed "anointed" here. And yet I think that even so he must be considered as a true "messianic" figure.

In essence, my reasoning is as follows. *4QTestimonia*, a collection of texts which the community interprets messianically, and corresponds to the three figures of 1QS IX 11, begins by quoting Deuteronomy 18:18–19 as the base text which is the foundation for hope in the "Prophet like Moses," "the Prophet" awaited at the end of time. Then comes Numbers 24:15–17, which is the foundation for the hope in the "Messiah-king." Then Deuteronomy 33:8–11, which is the foundation for hope in the "Messiah-priest." The three quotations are at the same level and in complete parallelism, and therefore must refer to similar figures. This figure of the "Prophet" is identical with the figures which the other texts denote as the "Interpreter of the Law," who "teaches justice at the end of times" and the "messenger"-figures which have a clear prophetic character and are considered as messianic figures. Like them, then, the "Prophet" must be considered as a "messianic" figure. About the last of these figures, "the messenger," we are told expressly in 11QMelch II 18 that he is "anointed by the spirit." In other words, the technical term which in 1QS IX 11 is applied to the other two "messianic" figures is applied to him, in the singular. Accordingly, it seems justifiable to consider this "Prophet," whose coming is expected at the same time as the "Messiahs of Aaron and of Israel," as a true "messianic" figure.

The first item in my argument is obvious and needs no explanation. Perhaps, though, it might be useful to note that "anointed" can be applied to the first of the three figures referred to by the biblical texts of this collection of *testimonia*, as well as to the other two. The choice of Deuteronomy 18:18–19 shows that the expected "Prophet" is a "Prophet like Moses." At Qumran, both Moses and the Prophets are called "anointed ones," a title which seems to be based on the parallel between "anointed ones" and "prophets" in Psalm 105:15 and in the Old Testament allusions to the "anointing" of prophets. The parallel with "seers" and the function of announcing and teaching which is attributed to them in the following two texts make it clear that the "anointed ones" spoken about are none other than the prophets. 1QM XI 7 runs: "By the hand of your anointed ones, seers of decrees, you taught us the times of the wars of your hands." And CD II 12: "And he taught them by the hands of his anointed ones[71] through his holy spirit and through seers of the truth." This allows CD VI 1 to be interpreted in the same way, where those who lead Israel astray rise against Moses but also against "the holy anointed ones." And in a still unpublished fragment of a pseudo-Mosaic composition, to be published by D. Dimant, can be read "through the mouth of Moses, his anointed one."[72] This seems to be nothing else than a description of Moses as a prophet.

It will be useful, perhaps, to quote the biblical text with which hope in his coming is justified, since it makes it clear that this expected prophet like Moses is portrayed in the biblical text as a true interpreter of the Law:

> ₅ "I would raise up for them a prophet from among their brothers, like you, and place my words ₆ in his mouth, and he would tell them all that I command them. And it will happen that the man ₇ who does not listen to my words, that the prophet will speak in my name, I ₈ shall require a reckoning from him." *Blank* (4Q175 5–8; DSST, 137).[73]

The second element is the most complex and implies examining the texts in which these figures occur. We have already quoted CD VII 18–21 and *4QFlorilegium* col. I 11–12, which portray the figure of the "Interpreter of the Law." But there is another text from the *Damascus Document* in which the same expression, "Interpreter of the Law," occurs again. It is CD VI 7, where the "staff" of Numbers 21:18 is identified as the "Interpreter of the Law," to whom the text of Isaiah 54:16 is applied. In this case, the wording and context of the text are sufficient proof that he is a person from the past. Most scholars identify him as the historical Teacher of Righteousness, also a person from the past.[74] One of the great merits of van der Woude's work is his convincing proof that both epithets "Interpreter of the Law" and "Teacher of Righteousness" are used as titles in CD. They are used to denote a person from the past and also an eschatological person whose coming is expected in the future. This enabled him to resolve the problem posed by the reference to an "Interpreter of the Law" in CD VI 7 as a figure from the past. He was also able to solve the problem posed by the text immediately after (in CD VI 11) which mentions a clearly eschatological figure from the future, given a title identical to that of "Teacher of Righteousness": "until there arises he who teaches justice at the end of days."

Van der Woude assembled the main arguments provided by the text proving that the historical figure referred to as "Teacher of Righteousness" and "Interpreter of the Law" was seen as a true "prophet." This allowed him to conclude that this historical figure had been perceived as a "Prophet like Moses," whose coming is expected in 1QS IX 11. In my view, this conclusion is wrong. A text such as CD XIX 35–XX 1 proves that the period of existence of the "unique Teacher" (or of the Teacher of the community) is seen as clearly different from the future coming of the "Messiahs" with whom the coming of the "Prophet" is associated.[75] However, his arguments to prove the prophetic character of the person are completely correct. And they prove that the figure called "Interpreter of the Law" or "he who teaches justice at the end of days" must be identified with this "Prophet," expected together with the "Messiahs of Aaron and of Israel." Precisely because the historical "Teacher of Righteousness" was perceived as a true prophet like Moses it was possible to use the titles "he who teaches justice" or "Interpreter of the Law" for this figure expected for the end of time and also described as a "Prophet" like Moses.

The fundamental difference between my way of seeing and van der Woude's is that for him the "Prophet" is not a "messianic" figure, but a forerunner of the Messiahs. I, on the other hand, believe that the eschatological "Prophet" is a "messianic" figure. He can only be identified with a historical person from the past if this person is considered as *redivivus*. His character of "messianic" figure is not an obstacle to his character of "forerunner." This appears to be proved by the third figure: the "messenger" whom 11QMelch describes together with the heavenly "Messiah," whose coming is expected in the final jubilee of history, and in the manuscript is called not only prophet but also "anointed by the spirit."

To complete this presentation of the texts it is necessary to include three references, one published and the other two from still unpublished manuscripts, which mention one or more "anointed ones." Unfortunately, the phrases lack a context which would allow their meaning to be determined. Yet, everything indicates that the first two refer not to a "Messiah" but to one or more "prophets." The person to whom the third reference applies cannot be determined.

The first reference occurs in 1Q30 fragment 1,2[76] and the reading is very uncertain: "[an]ointed of holiness." The parallelism with the expression of CD VI 1 and the possible reference of line 4 to "the five books" suggest that it applies to a prophet.

The second reference is in the last line of a column, the only line preserved in fragment 10 of 4Q287.[77] The work from which it comes is a collection of blessings and curses of which several copies have been found and from which Milik had published a few lines.[78] According to the transcription of the line in question in the *Preliminary Concordance*, the phrase should be translated "the holy spirit [res]ted upon his anointed one." However, the reading is uncertain. In fact, the photograph allows reading the plural "his anointed ones," and the parallel in CD II 12 requires the translation: "upon the anointed ones of the spirit of holiness," i.e., the prophets.

We cannot conclude anything either from another recently published text in which the phrase "anointed with the oil of kingship"[79] occurs. This is because we do not know to whom it refers. In the fragment where it occurs (frag. 2 of 4Q458[80]) someone destroys someone else and devours the uncircumcised, so that the phrase could have been applied to the expected "king-Messiah." However, all that can be concluded is that it expresses the royal anointing of the person to whom it refers, whoever that person might be.

The simple presentation of the "messianic" texts has turned out to be too lengthy to allow us now to try and summarise the data they provide as a form of conclusion. In addition, I am not certain that a summary like J. Starcky's famous summary,[81] in which he discovered four stages of development in the Qumran community, would be possible today. The famous omission of the messianic passage 1QS IX 11 from the oldest copy, palaeographically speaking, of the *Rule*, if not due to accidental causes, suggests a certain development. And the palaeographically late date (1st century CE) of the two texts which mention the heavenly "Messiah" could indicate that this form of messianic hope is a later development. However, these simple facts do not allow a summary to be attempted. Even, for example, a summary which, starting with the clear biblical antecedents of the idea of a davidic Messiah, and going on to a priestly Messiah, double messianism, the multiplication of expected messianic figures (whether called "Messiah" or not) culminates in the hope for a heavenly "Messiah."

I am not even convinced that it would be possible to fit all these texts into G. Scholem's scheme of a "restorative messianism" versus a "utopian messianism" as Talmon and Schiffman do.[82] This does not necessarily imply the conclusion that for the Qumran community "messianic" ideas were a private matter, in which different and even conflicting opinions could co-exist in harmony because ultimately they lack importance,[83] or because in "messianology" consistency is impossible.[84] The large number of references inserted in every kind of literary context, including legal contexts, testifies to its importance for the Qumran community. And the hope in many and varied "messianic" figures cannot be considered as itself "inconsistent." Ultimately, in the 1st century the Jewish group whom we know through the New Testament was to merge the hope in a "Messiah king," a "Messiah-priest," a "Prophet like Moses," a "Suffering Servant" and even a "heavenly Messiah" into one historical person from the past whose return is expected in the eschatological future.

## Notes

1. Written at the request of Professor Gunter Sternberger and published in German in the *Jahrbuch für Biblische Theologie* 8 (1993).

2. From the basic work by A. S. van der Woude, *Die messianische Vorstellungen der Gemeinde von Qumran* (Studia Semitica Neerlandica 3) Assen 1957. A bibliography of the most important works from these twenty-five years is to be found in J. A. Fitzmyer, *The Dead Sea Scrolls. Major Publications and Tools for Study* (Society of Biblical Literature [SBL] Resources for Biblical Study 4) Missoula 1975, 114–118.

3. It is significant that in the 1991 edition of his *The Dead Sea Scrolls. Major Publications and Tools for Study* (SBL Resources for Biblical Study 20) Atlanta 1991, 164–167 adds only six titles to the list published in 1975.

4. Among the studies published recently see G. J. Brooke, "The Messiah of Aaron in the Damascus Document," *Revue de Qumrân (RQ)* 15/57–58 (1991) 215–230; A. Chester, "Jewish Messianic Expectations and Mediatorial Figures and Pauline Christology," in M. Hengel-U. Heckel (eds.), *Paulus und das antike Judentum*, Tübingen 1992, 17–89; M. A. Knibb, "The Teacher of Righteousness—A Messianic Title?" in P. R. Davies-R. T. White (eds.), *A Tribute to Geza Vermes* (JSOT Press 100) Sheffield 1990, 51–65; M. A. Knibb, "The Interpretation of *Damascus Document* VII, 9b-VIII, 2a and XIX, 5b–14," *RQ* 15/57–58 (1991) 243–251; P. Sacchi, "Esquisse du développement du messianisme juif à la lumière du texte qumrânien 11QMelch," *Zeitschrift für die Alttestamentliche Wissenschaft (ZAW)* 100 (Supplement) (1988)

202–214; F. M. Schweitzer, "The Teacher of Righteousness," in Z. J. Kapera (ed.), *Mogilany 1989. Papers on the Dead Sea Scrolls,* Volume 2 (Qumranica Mogilanensia 3), Kraków 1991, 53–97; L. E. Schiffman, "Messianic Figures and Ideas in the Qumran Scrolls," in J. H. Charlesworth (ed.), *The Messiah. Developments in Early Judaism and Christianity,* Minneapolis 1992, 116–129; S. Talmon, "Waiting for the Messiah—The Conceptual Universe of the Qumran Covenanters," in S. Talmon (ed.), *The World of Qumran from Within. Collected Studies,* Jerusalem/Leiden 1989, 273–300 (= J. Neusner-W. S. Green-E. Frerichs (eds.), *Judaisms and Their Messiahs at the Turn of the Christian Era,* Cambridge 1987, 111–137); S. Talmon, "The Concept of Māšîaḥ and Messianism in Early Judaism," in J. H. Charlesworth (ed.), *The Messiah,* 79–115; J. C. VanderKam, "Jubilees and the Priestly Messiah of Qumran," *RQ* 13/49–52 (1988) 353–365.

5. They are the *editio princeps* of three Aramaic texts completed by E. Puech, "Fragment d'une apocalypse en araméen (4Q246 = pseudo-Dan) et le 'Royaume de Dieu,' " *Revue biblique (RB)* 99 (1992) 98–131; "Une apocalypse messianique (4Q521)," *RQ* 15/60 (1992) 475–522; "Fragments d'un apocryphe de Lévi et le personnage eschatologique. 4QTestLévi[a-d](?) et 4QAJ," in J. Trebolle-Barrera-L. Vegas Montaner (eds.), *The Madrid Qumran Congress* (Studies on the Texts of the Desert of Judah [STDJ] 11) Leiden 1992, 449–501, pls. 16–22; and of a Hebrew fragment published by G. Vermes, "The Oxford Forum for Qumran Research: Seminar on the Rule of War from Cave 4 (4Q285)," *Journal of Jewish Studies (JJS)* 43 (1992) 85–94.

6. For example, L. H. Schiffman in "Messianic Figures and Ideas in the Qumran Scrolls" (cited in note 4).

7. In Hesse's words, "Keine der Messias-Stellen des Alten Testaments kann messianisch gedeutet werden," *Theologisches Wörterbuch zum Neuen Testament* IX, 494.

8. In which the Blessing of Jacob comprises one of the key texts for the expression of messianic hope. See the detailed study by M. Pérez Fernández, *Tradiciones mesiánicas en el Targum Palestinense,* Jerusalem-Valencia 1981, 112–144, especially pp. 123–135 on Genesis 49:10.

9. The messianic passage was published by J. M. Allegro, "Further Messianic References in Qumran Literature," *Journal of Biblical Literature (JBL)* 75 (1956) 74–184; the first two preserved columns of the manuscript have been published recently by T. H. Lim, "The Chronology of the Flood Story in a Qumran Text (4Q252)," *JJS* 43 (1992) 288–298. The photographs of all the fragments preserved is to be found in PAM 43.253 and 43.381, reproduced in plates 1289 and 1375 of R. H. Eisenman-J. M. Robinson (eds.), *A Facsimile Edition of the Dead Sea Scrolls (FE)*, Biblical Archaeological Society, Washington 1991.

10. Separated by a *Blank* in the foregoing text and with the heading "Jacob's Blessings" in 4Q252 IV 3.

11. Column IV 3–7 contains remains of the blessing of Reuben, V 1–7, part of the blessing of Judah and the remains of column VI correspond to the blessing of Naphtali.

12. The actual quotation has not been preserved and it is impossible to know whether a literal quotation from Genesis 49:10 preceded the commentary of this column V. The evidence of the preceding columns is ambiguous in this regard; the blessing of Reuben begins with the literal quotation followed by its *pesher*, but the interpretation, for example, of the story of the flood is incorporated into the additions, changes and omissions of the actual account.

13. As van der Woude had already proved (op. cit. in note 2) 171–172.

14. 4Q254 (4QpGen$^c$): PAM, 43.233, *FE* 1270.

15. Q253 (4QpGen$^b$): PAM, 43.258, *FE* 1294.

16. Text in J. M. Allegro, *Discoveries in the Judaean Desert of Jordan (DJD)* V, Oxford 1968, 11–15, plates 4–5, with the corrections by J. Strugnell, "Notes en marge du volume V des 'Discoveries in the Judaean Desert of Jordan,' " *RQ* 7 (1969–71) 183–186.

17. A title which, in itself, seems to identify its bearer as the davidic "Messiah" in so far as it obviously derives from the "Prince" of Ezekiel 40–48, the chief of the future community, of which Ezekiel 34:24 and 37:25 says precisely "and my servant David will be his prince for ever."

18. Published by J. T. Milik in *Discoveries in the Judaean Desert (DJD)* I, Oxford 1955, 118–130, pls. 25–29.

19. 4Q285 and the copy which comes from Cave 11, published by A. S. van der Woude with the title *11QBerakhot*, "Ein neuer Segensspruch aus Qumran," in *Bibel und Qumran* (Festschrift H. Bardtke), Berlin 1968, 253–258, which matches fragments 3 and 4 of 4Q285. This match was noticed by J. T. Milik, "Milkîṣedeq and Milkî-rešaˁ dans les anciens écrits juifs et chrétiens," *JJS* 23 (1972): 143, who was also the first to suggest that both manuscripts come from the lost ending to the *War Rule*.

20. Besides fragment 5,4 there are references to the "Prince of the congregation" in fragments 4.2 and 6,2; unfortunately, though, they are references which are too fragmentary to provide us with any useful elements.

21. G. Vermes, "The Oxford Forum for Qumran Research: Seminar or the Rule of War from Cave 4(4Q285)" (cited in note 5).

22. J. D. Tabor, "A Pierced or Piercing Messiah?—The Verdict is Still Out," *Biblical Archaeology Review (BAR)* 18/6 (1992) 58–59

23. Besides the texts quoted, the "Prince of the congregation" occurs in IQM V 1, where only tells us the inscription he will bear on his sceptre, and in CD 7,20 and 4Q376, two texts we will study below.

24. E. Puech, "Une apocalypse messianique" (cited in note 5).

25. J. Starcky, in "Le travail d'édition des manuscrits de Qumrân," *RB* 63 (1956) 66.

26. In fragment 9,3 the word "Messiah" is incomplete, so that it cannot be used.

27. A unique expression and difficult to explain, given that in the other writings it is always a matter of God's "precepts" and in most cases God is explicitly mentioned. In the Qumran texts, as in the Hebrew Bible, "Holy Ones" could evidently denote the angels. Accordingly, the phrase could mean the union of the "Messiah" with the "Holy Ones" and indicate that in the messianic age all creation will keep the angelic precepts. However, "the holy ones" is also used (especially in texts of eschatological content, such as 1QM and 1QSb) to denote the members of the community,

so that the expression could be understood as alluding to the divine precepts exactly as they are interpreted by the members of the community. Or is it merely an objective adjective for these precepts as holy precepts?

28. In fact, the reference to "all Israel" in III 5 could imply a different context since the author appears to restrict his horizon to the faithful members of the community in the description of the messianic age of column II. In the allusion to the sceptre a reference to the "Messiah of Israel," and in the allusions to the priesthood of fragments 8–9, Puech accepts a possible reference to the "priestly Messiah," but prudently concludes that the condition of the manuscript does not permit any definitive conclusion.

29. M. O. Wise-J. D. Tabor, "The Messiah at Qumran," *BAR* 18/6 (1992) 60–65.

30. Although they accept that it is a purely speculative reconstruction.

31. As specified in fragment 7+5 II 5–6: "like these, the accursed; and they shall be for death [when] (6) [he makes] the dead of his people [ri]se."

32. E. Puech, "Fragments d'un apocryphe de Lévi et le personnage eschatologique. 4QTestLévi$^{a-d}$(?) et 4QAJ" (cited in note 5).

33. J. Starcky, "Les quatre étapes du messianisme à Qumran," *RB* 70 (1963) 492.

34. "And after vengeance on them will have come from the Lord, the priesthood will fail. Then the Lord will raise up a new priest, to whom all the words of the Lord will be revealed; and he will execute a judgment of truth upon the earth in course of time. And his star will arise in heaven, as a king, lighting up the light of knowledge as by the sun of the day; and he will be magnified in the world until his assumption. He will shine as the sun on the earth and will remove all darkness from under heaven, and there will be peace on all the earth," TestLev 18:1–4, as translated by H. W. Hollander-M. de Jonge, *The Testaments of the Twelve Pariarchs* (Studia inVeteris Testamenti Pseudepigrapha 8) Leiden 1985, 177.

35. See recently J. C. VanderKam, "Righteous One, Messiah, Chosen One, and Son of Man in I Enoch 3–71" in J. H. Charlesworth (ed.), *The Messiah* (cited in note 4) 169–191, with references to previous studies.

36. M. Stone, "The Question of the Messiah in 4 Ezra," in M. Stone, *Selected Studies in Pseudepigrapha & Apocrypha* (Studia Varsaviensia theologica papers 9) 317–322(=J. Neusner-W. S. Green-E. Frerich [eds.], *Judaism and Their Messiahs at the Turn of the Christian Era*, Cambridge 1987, 209–224) and "Excursus on the Redeemer Figure," in M. Stone, *Fourth Ezra* (Hermeneia), Minneapolis 1990, 207–213.

37. In an excellent article in which he stresses how both figures represent a particular "messianic" interpretation of Daniel 7, "The Son of Man in First-Century Judaism," *New Testament Studies (NTS)* 38 (1992) 448–466. Collins suggests (p. 466 note 78) that 4Q246 could contain a similar messianic interpretation of the Daniel figure, an intuition which seems absolutely correct and matches my own understanding of the text.

38. The text was presented by J. T. Milik in a lecture given at Harvard University in 1972 and was made known by J. A. Fitzmyer in his study "The Contribution of Qumran Aramaic to the Study of the New Testament," *NTS* 20 (1972–74) 382–407 and reprinted with an important supplement in J. A. Fitzmyer, *A Wandering Aramean. Collected Aramaic Essays* (SBL Monograph Series 25), Chico 1979, 85–107.

39. See D. Flusser, "The Hubris of the Antichrist in a Fragment from Qumran," *Immanuel* 10 (1980) 31–37, and F. García Martínez, "The eschatological figure of 4Q246" in F. García Martínez, *Qumran and Apocalyptic* (STDJ 9) Leiden 1992, 162–179. G. Kuhn, "Röm 1,3 f und der davidische Messias als Gottessohn in den Qumrantexten," in Ch. Burchard-G. Thiessen (eds.), *Lese-Zeichen für Annelies Findreiß zum 65. Geburtstag am 15. März 1984*, Heidelberg 1984, 103–113.

40. E. Puech, "Fragment d'une apocalypse en araméen (4Q246 = pseudo-Dan[d]) et le 'Royaume de Dieu' " (cited above, note 5).

41. F. García Martínez, "The eschatological figure of 4Q246" (note 39).

42. E. Puech, 124–125 and 102, note 14.

43. On the interpretation of the "Son of Man" of Daniel 7 as an individual with an angelic nature see J. J. Collins, *The Apocalyptic Vision of the Book of Daniel* (Harvard Semitic Monographs 16) Ann Arbor 1977, 144–147.

44. See E. Puech, 116–117.

45. *Ibid.* 129.

46. Edition and plates in *The Dead Sea Scrolls of St. Mark's Monastery*, Vol. II, New Haven 1951. Colour photographs by J. C. Trever in *Scrolls from Qumran Cave 1*, Jerusalem 1972. I have also been able to use a new critical edition prepared by E. Qimron which includes the parallels from the copies from other caves, to be published shortly.

47. For a general view of the messianism of this work see A. S. van der Woude, *Die messianische Vorstellungen* (cited in note 2) 190–216.

48. A detail made known by J. T. Milik, *Ten Years of Discovery in the Wilderness of Judaea*, London 1959, 123–124 and in *RB* 67 (1960) 413 and exploited by J. Starcky in his famous article "Les quatres étapes du messianisme à Qumrân" (cited in note 33).

49. 4Q259 col. III 6; see PAM 43.263, *FE* 1299.

50. I use the critical edition prepared by E. Qimron and included in M. Broshi (ed.), *The Damascus Document Reconsidered*, Jerusalem 1992, which is accompanied by photographs of excellent quality and contains parallels to the copies found in Qumran.

51. The phrase occurs in the oldest copy of CD from Cave 4, 4Q266 (4QDo.11a) frag. 18 III 12, which proves that it is an original reading and not a correction by a medieval copyist; see PAM 43.276, *FE* 1312.

52. The manuscript reads *meshuach*, an obvious mistake as all scholars accept.

53. Although the copy 4QD$^b$ frag. 18 III 1 (PAM 43.270, *FE* 1306) reads "Messiah of Aaron and Israel."

54. See most recently the article by G. Brooke cited in note 4.

55. F. M. Cross, "Some Notes on a Generation of Qumran Studies," in *The Madrid Qumran Congress*, (STDJ XI/1) Leiden

1992, 14 frames this trenchant conclusion: "The putative single messiah is a phantom of bad philology."

56. Edition and plates in DJD I, Oxford 1955, 108–118, pls. 23–24. The only monograph devoted entirely to this manuscript is L. H. Schiffman, *The Eschatological Community of the Dead Sea Scrolls* (Society of Biblical Literature Monograph Series 38) Atlanta 1989.

57. DJD I, 117. See also P. Skehan, "Two Books on Qumran Studies," *Catholic Biblical Quarterly* 21 (1959) 74. For other readings and interpretations see K. G. Kuhn, "The Two Messiahs of Aaron and Israel," in K. Stendahl, *The Scrolls and the New Testament*, London 1958, 56 or L. H. Schiffman, *op. cit.* (previous note) 54, who follows the readings and reconstructions of J. Licht.

58. See, for example, A. S. van der Woude (*op. cit.* note 2) 101–104 and L. H. Schiffman (*op. cit.* note 56) 55–56. This conclusion forces this same messianic figure to be acknowledged in the "Chief Priest" or "High Priest" of 1QM II 1; XV 4 and XVI 13, as van der Woude already has, against what L. Schiffman explicitly states on p. 123 of the article cited in note 4. Even more than in 4Q285, which apparently comes from the end of the same composition, the "Prince of the congregation" plays an important role and as we have seen above, this name is one of the titles of the "davidic Messiah." Discussion of these texts, however, must be reserved for another occasion.

59. J. Strugnell, "Moses-Pseudepigrapha at Qumran: 4Q375, 4Q376, and Similar Works," in L. H. Schiffman (ed.), *Archaeology and History in the Dead Sea Scrolls*, The New York Conference in Memory of Yigael Yadin (*Journal for the Study of the Pseudepigrapha* 8) Sheffield 1990, 221–256.

60. The two most characteristic allusions in terms of vocabulary to indicate a Qumran origin of the composition, "hidden things" and "fathers of the congregation," are partly reconstructions by the editor.

61. The text is found in part in the copy 4QD$^b$ (4Q267) frag. 3 col. IV 9–10 (PAM 43.270, *FE* 1306) and possibly in 4Q271, 4QD$^f$ frag. 5 (PAM 43.300, *FE* 1335) although this is very uncertain.

62. As, for example, A. Caquot, "Le messianisme qumrânien" in M. Delcor (ed.), *Qumrân: Sa piété, sa théologie et son milieu* (Bibliotheca Ephemeridum Theologicarum Lovaniensium 46) Louvain 1978, 241–242.

63. For example, G. Brooke, "The Amos-Numbers Midrash (CD 7,13b–8) and Messianic Expectation," *ZAW* 92 (1980) 397–404. See most recently the detailed study of the passage by M. Knibb in *RQ* 15/57–58 (1991) 248–251 (cited in note 4).

64. J. Starcky, "Les quatres étapes" (cited in note 33), 497.

65. In the work cited in note 2, 43–61 and in his contribution to the IX[es] Journées Bibliques de Louvain, "Le Maître de Justice et les deux messies de la communauté de Qumrân" in *La secte de Qumrân et les origines chrétiennes* (Recherches Bibliques 4) Bruges 1969, 123–134.

66. See most recently P. Pilhofer, "Wer salbt den Messias? Zum Streit um die Chronologie im ersten Jahrhundert des jüdisch-christlichen Dialogs," in D.-A. Koch-H. Lichtenberger (eds.), *Begegnungen zwischen Christentum und Judentum in Antike und Mittelalter* (Festschrift für H. Schrekenberg), Göttingen 1993, 335–345.

67. N. Wieder, "The Doctrine of the two Messiahs among the Karaites," *JJS* 6 (1953) 14–23.

68. Text and plates in DJD V, Oxford 1968, 53–57, pls. 19–20.

69. The manuscript was published by A. S. van der Woude, "Melchisedek als himmlische Erlösergestalt in den neugefundenen eschatologischen Midraschim aus Qumran Höhle XI," *Oudtestamentische Studien* 14 (1963) 354–373, 2. pls., and has been extensively studied. My translation incorporates most of the readings and reconstructions proposed by E. Puech, "Notes sur le manuscrit de 11QMelkisédeq," *RQ* 12/48 (1987) 483–513.

70. As the editor explained in a joint article with M. de Jonge, "11QMelchizedek and the New Testament," *NTS* 12 (1966) 307.

71. The correction of the text from "his anointed one" to "anointed ones" is generally accepted.

72. 4Q377 2 II 5 *FE* 497, a central fragment with remains of two columns. Unfortunately, this photograph, the only one available

to me, is of such bad quality that the fragment remains virtually unreadable. The manuscript is labelled Sl 12 in the *Preliminary Concordance to the Hebrew and Aramaic Fragments from Qumrân Caves II-X*, where the phrase in question is transcribed.

73. Text and plates in DJD V, Oxford 1968, 57–60, pl. 21.

74. See the arguments adduced by van der Woude in the works cited in note 67. This figure occurs frequently in 1QpHab and in CD, where he is called "Teacher of Righteousness," "Unique Teacher," "he who teaches justice" or "the unique teacher" interchangeably.

75. A fact which van der Woude accepts but resolves by supposing that the text of 1QS IX 11, which witnesses the hope in the "Prophet" is earlier than the appearance of the Teacher of Righteousness his acceptance? as prophet and his death; see *Die messianische Vorstellungen*, 84–85 and 187.

76. Text and plates in DJD I, 132–133, pl. 30.

77. PAM 43,400; *FE* 1394.

78. J. T. Milik "Milki-ṣedeq et Milki-reša‘" (cited in note 19) 130–131.

79. (See DSST, 228ff.). The phrase is cited by Strugnell (article cited in note 59) as parallel to the expression "oil of anointing" in 4Q375 I 8, and to "oil of his priestly anointing" in 1QM IX 8, and as coming from 4Q453 2 II 6. The work has now been given the siglum 4Q458.

80. PAM 43.544; *FE* 1493.

81. In his article "Les quatre étapes du messianisme à Qumrân" (cited in note 33).

82. In the studies cited in note 4.

83. As M. Smith, "What is implied in the variety of messianic figures," *JBL* 78 (1959) 66–72 seems to suggest.

84. As J. H. Charlesworth "From Messianology to Christology. Problems and Prospects," in *The Messiah*, 28, concludes.

# CHAPTER 6

# THE BOOK OF MORMON AND THE DEAD SEA SCROLLS

*Stephen D. Ricks*

Consider this tale of two peoples:

The individuals of one group, originally a family,

- left their mother city, Jerusalem, because they believed that it was becoming irredeemably wicked and that it would eventually be destroyed;

- went out into the desert in order to escape its corruption;

- having left the desert, built temples and had priests;

- strictly observed the law of Moses;

- required the complete immersion of those who entered their community;

- looked forward with anxious anticipation to the coming of their Messiah; and

- wrote on metal plates that they hid away in a time of crisis.

---

*Stephen D. Ricks is professor of Hebrew and Semitic languages at Brigham Young University and chairman of the FARMS Board of Trustees.*

The other group also

- left Jerusalem, which they, too, believed had become irretrievably corrupted;
- withdrew into the desert to escape its corruption;
- loved the temple and honored priests as members of their community;
- strictly observed the law of Moses;
- required immersion of those who wished to enter their community;
- looked forward with eager anticipation for the coming of their Messiah(s); and
- wrote on parchment, on papyrus, and in one case on metal plates, which they hid away in a time of crisis.

Which groups fit these descriptions? The group first described was Lehi and his family, who left Jerusalem and escaped into the desert around 600 B.C. because Lehi had been warned by the Lord that Jerusalem would be destroyed (see 1 Nephi 1:4, 13; 3:17; 2 Nephi 1:4). In the New World, the Nephites built temples that formed the center of their communities (see 2 Nephi 5:16; Jacob 1:17; 2:2, 11; Helaman 3:9, 14). They observed the law of Moses (see 2 Nephi 25:24; Jacob 4:5; 7:7; Jarom 1:5, 11; Mosiah 2:3) while looking forward to the coming of their Messiah (see 2 Nephi 25:16, 18; Jarom 1:11). They organized a church (see Mosiah 21:30; 26:17; Helaman 3:24–5) that required baptism of all those wishing to become members (see Mosiah 18:16–7). The Nephites wrote their history on metal plates (see the title page of the Book of Mormon; 1 Nephi 1:17; Mosiah 1:3–4, 6; Omni 1:3–4, 8, 11; Mormon 1:4; 2:18), which the last of the Nephites, Moroni, hid to come forth "in their purity" at a later time (see 1 Nephi 14:26).

Members of the second group included the writers of many of the Dead Sea Scrolls, who also left Jerusalem (probably sometime in the late third or early second century B.C.),[1] established a home in the wilderness, loved the temple, honored priests and Levites,[2] expected the imminent coming of their Messiah(s),[3] and wrote on various materials, including parchment, papyrus, and copper plates, which they buried in haste in a time of danger to the community.[4]

Professor Stephen D. Ricks outside Qumran Cave 3.

## The Dead Sea Scrolls and the Book of Mormon: A Comparison

The correlation between the actions of these two groups of people is not the only similarity. A study of the theological themes in the documents they produced reveals several common topics in their beliefs.[5]

1. The writings of the community of the Dead Sea Scrolls reveal a strong sense of being a covenant people, who saw themselves as the continuation of the true Israel. Compare the ideas in the following quotations from the scrolls with the feelings of the peoples of the Book of

Mormon, who saw themselves as a "remnant of the house of Israel" (title page of the Book of Mormon):

> {W}elcome into the covenant of kindness all those who freely volunteer to carry out God's decrees, so as to be united in the counsel of God and walk in perfection in his sight, complying with all revealed things concerning the regulated times of their stipulations. (1QS I 7–9)

> And all those who enter in the Rule of the Community shall establish a covenant before God in order to carry out all that he commands and in order not to stray from following him for any fear, dread or grief that might occur during the dominion of Belial. When they enter the covenant, the priests and the levites shall bless the God of salvation and all the works of his faithfulness and all those who enter the covenant shall repeat after them: 'Amen, Amen.' (1QS I 16–20)

> [And all] those who enter the covenant shall confess after
>     them and they shall say:
> "We have acted sinfully,
> [we have transgressed,
> we have si]nned, we have acted irreverently,
> we and our fathers before us,
> inasmuch as we walk
> [in the opposite direction to the precepts] of truth and
>     justice
> [. . .] his judgment upon us and upon our fathers."
>                                  (1QS I 24–6)

> And all those who enter the covenant shall say, after those
>     who pronounce
> blessings and those who pronounce curses: "Amen, Amen."
> *Blank* And the priests and the levites shall continue, saying:
> . . .
> "whoever enters this covenant

leaving his guilty obstacle in front of himself
to fall over it.
When he hears the words of this covenant,
he will congratulate himself in his heart, saying:
'I will have peace.'

(1QS II 10–3)

May all the curses of this covenant
stick fast to him.
May God segregate him for evil,
and may he be cut off from the midst of all the sons of
    light
because of his straying from following God
on account of his idols and his blameworthy obstacle.
May he assign his lot with the cursed ones for ever.

(1QS II 16–7)[6]

2.   The writers of the Dead Sea Scrolls insisted on strict observance of the law of Moses, including a particular concern for the time and manner of observing the festivals. The members of the Dead Sea community intended to live "the law which he commanded through the hand of Moses" (1QS VIII 15). Compare the following quotations from the scrolls to 2 Nephi 25:24, where Nephi says that they "keep the law of Moses" even though they "believe in Christ" and "look forward with steadfastness . . . until the law shall be fulfilled":

> For [the Instructor . . .] . . . [book of the Rul]e of the Community: in order to seek God [with all (one's) heart and with all (one's) soul; in order] to do what is good and just in his presence, as commanded by means of the hand of Moses and his servants the Prophets; in order to love everything which he selects and to hate everything that he rejects; in order to keep oneself at a distance from all evil, and to become attached to all good works; to bring about truth, justice and uprightness. (1QS I 1–5)

As it is written: "In the desert, prepare the way of {the Lord}, straighten in the steppe a roadway for our God." This is the study of the law which he commanded through the hand of Moses, in order to act in compliance with all that has been revealed from age to age, and according to what the prophets have revealed through his holy spirit. (1QS VIII 14–6)

And he taught them by the hand of the anointed ones through his holy spirit and through seers of the truth, and their names were established with precision. (CD II 12–3)

3. Writers from both these groups display a vivid sense of expectation of the coming of the Messiah. Like the early Christians, they lived in the belief that the end of days was at hand and that their struggle was with the principalities and powers, and they reinterpreted the scriptures in that context. According to one eminent scholar in the field, Professor Frank Moore Cross, "Theirs was a church of anticipation."[7] Many of the Dead Sea Scrolls, such as the *Rule of the Congregation* (or *Messianic Rule*), are written in expectation of the time when the Messiah would be present in their midst or (in the case of the *Temple Scroll*) of an era immediately preceding the Messianic age. The Book of Mormon, too, reveals an intense expectation of the coming of their Messiah (usually referred to in the Book of Mormon as Christ).[8] The Nephites "look forward unto Christ [i.e., the Messiah] with steadfastness for the signs which are given"(2 Nephi 26:8). Indeed, the prophets of the Book of Mormon even prophesy the year of Christ's birth: Nephi prophesies that Christ will be born "six hundred years from the time that my father left Jerusalem" (1 Nephi 10:4), while the mysterious Samuel the Lamanite tells the Nephites that he would be born in five years (Helaman 14:2).

Examine the strong messianic expectations in the following excerpts from the scrolls:

> For he will honour the devout upon the throne of eternal royalty, freeing prisoners, giving sight to the blind, straightening out the twisted. Ever shall I cling to those who hope. In his mercy he will jud[ge,] and from no-one shall the fruit [of] good [deeds] be delayed, and the Lord will perform marvellous acts such as have not existed, just as he sa[id] for he will heal the badly wounded and will make the dead live, he will proclaim good news to the meek give lavishly [to the need]y, lead the exiled and enrich the hungry. (4Q521 II 7–13)

> And they will recount the splendour of his kingdom, according to their knowledge, and they will extol [his glory in all] the heavens of his kingdom. And in all the exalted heights [they will sing] wonderful psalms according to all [their knowledge,] and they will tell [of the splendour] of the glory of the king of the gods in the residences of their positions. (4Q400 2 i 3–5)

> He will be called son of God, and they will call him son of the Most High. Like the sparks of a vision, so will their kingdom be; they will rule several years over the earth and crush everything; a people will crush another people, and a city another city. *Blank* Until the people of God arises and makes everyone rest from the sword. His kingdom will be an eternal kingdom, and all his paths in truth and uprigh[tness]. (4Q246 II 1–5)

> A star has departed from Jacob, /and/ a sceptre /has arisen/ from Israel. He shall crush the temples of Moab, and cut to pieces all the sons of Sheth. (4Q175 12–3)

4. Temples played a vitally important role among the peoples of the Book of Mormon. Following their arrival in the promised land, Nephi built a temple "after the manner of the temple of Solomon save it were not built of so many

precious things" (2 Nephi 5:16), where Nephi's brothers Jacob and Joseph later taught as priests (see Jacob 1:17–8). Subsequently, temples were built in Zarahemla (see Mosiah 1:18, 2:1, 5–7) and in Bountiful, where the risen Christ appeared to the people (see 3 Nephi 11:1; compare Mosiah 6:3).[9]

The writers of the Dead Sea Scrolls also placed great importance on the priesthood and the temple:

> In the Community council (there shall be) twelve men and three priests, perfect in everything that has been revealed about all the law to implement truth, justice, judgment, compassionate love and unassuming behaviour of each person to his fellow to preserve faithfulness on the earth with firm purpose and repentant spirit in order to atone for sin, doing justice and undergoing trials in order to walk with everyone in the measure of truth and the regulation of time. (1QS VIII 1–4)

> {A}t this moment the men of the Community shall set themselves apart (like) a holy house for Aaron, in order to enter the holy of holies, and (like) a house of the Community for Israel, (for) those who walk in perfection. (1QS IX 5–6)

> They shall not desecrate the oil of their priestly anointing with the blood of futile nations. (1QM IX 8–9)

> And the priests, sons of Aaron, shall station themselves in front of the lines and blow the memorial trumpets. And afterwards, they shall open the gat[es] to the soldiers of the infantry. The priests shall blow the battle trumpets [to strike] the lines of the nations. (4Q493 1–4)

> They shall be for me a people and I will be for them for ever and I shall establish them for ever and always. I shall sanctify my temple with my glory, for I shall make my glory reside over it until the day of creation, when I shall

create my temple, establishing it for myself for ever, in accordance with the covenant which I made with Jacob at Bethel. (11Q19 XXIX 7–9)

[Because he has established] the holy of holies among the eternal holy ones, so that for him they can be priests [who approach the temple of his kingship,] the servants of the Presence in the sanctuary of his glory. In the assembly of all the deities [of knowledge, and in the council of all the spirits] of God, he has engraved his ordinances for all spiritual works, and his [glorious] precepts [for those who establish] knowledge of the people of the intelligence of his glory, the gods who approach knowledge. (4Q400 1 i 3–6)

Priests and Levites played a crucial role in the organization and operation of the Qumran community. Although the temple in Jerusalem was seen as corrupt, the writers of the Qumran scrolls had a vision of a purified interim temple as well as a temple of the endtime.

5.  Passages from the Dead Sea Scrolls and the Book of Mormon reflect the belief that a war is being waged between good and evil. Both show a strong sense that good will prevail. Compare Alma 12:31; 29:5; and Moroni 7:19 to the following:

And in the hand of the Angel of Darkness is total dominion over the sons of deceit; they walk on paths of darkness. Due to the Angel of Darkness all the sons of justice stray, and all their sins, their iniquities, their failings and their mutinous deeds are under his dominion in compliance with the mysteries of God, until his moment; and all their punishments and their periods of grief are caused by the dominion of his enmity. (1QS III 20–3)

{T}o separate themselves from the sons of the pit; to abstain from wicked wealth which defiles, either by promise or by vow, and from the wealth of the temple and from stealing from the poor of the people, from making their widows their spoils and from murdering orphans; to separate unclean from clean and differentiate between the holy and the common. (CD VI 14–7)

The sons of light and the lot of darkness shall battle together for God's might, between the roar of a huge multitude and the shout of gods and of men, on the day of the calamity. It will be a time of suffering fo[r al]l the people redeemed by God. (1QM I 11–2)

Since ancient time you determined the day of the great
    battle
[…] to assist truth,
and destroy wickedness,
to demolish darkness
and increase light.

(1QM XIII 14–5)

Do not all peoples loathe sin?
And yet, they all walk about under its influence.
Does not praise of truth come from the mouth of all nations?
And yet, is there perhaps one lip or one tongue which
    persists with it?

(1Q27 1 i 9–10)

## Conclusion

Qumran illustrates the presence of prophecy in one Jewish group, which believed that it lived the last days—a time within which the gift of prophecy had been renewed. The community as a whole was convinced that the Spirit of God, an eschatological gift, was present and active in their midst in providing "cleansing, truth, holiness, and divinely mediated knowledge and insight."[10] According to Josephus, among the Essenes "there are some . . . who profess to foretell the future, being versed from their early years in holy books, various forms of purification and apothegms of prophets; and seldom, if ever, do they err in their predictions."[11] The writers of the Dead Sea Scrolls believe in the inspired interpretation of scripture and prophecy. The *Commentary on Habakkuk* faults those who do not believe the words of the Teacher of Righteousness, who says that he received "from the mouth of God."[12] Book of Mormon prophets taught that the scriptures were "plain unto all those that are filled with the spirit of prophecy" (2 Nephi 25:4; see also verse 7), and that the spirit of prophecy and revelation was in their midst (see Alma 17:3).

Of course, there are differences between the Book of Mormon and the Dead Sea Scrolls: the desert was the final destination of the writers of the Dead Sea Scrolls, not the transit point as for Lehi and his family. The writers of the

Ruins of Qumran on the northwestern shore of the Dead Sea. The map on page 119 identifies the various areas of the settlement. (Photograph by Werner Braun.)

Dead Sea Scrolls loved the temple but did not build their own, while the Nephites did. Although both peoples observed the law of Moses, only the Nephites in the Book of Mormon looked forward to its fulfillment in Christ. Still, the areas of overlap between these people and the contours of correspondence between them—their warm belief in prophecy, their vivid sense of living in the end time, their belief in being a covenant people, the true remnant of Israel—help us to understand the good tidings that have come since Cumorah about those things that were held sacred in antiquity.

## Notes

1. See Lawrence H. Schiffman, *Reclaiming the Dead Sea Scrolls: Their True Meaning for Judaism and Christianity* (New York: Doubleday, 1995), 83–95; compare Hartmut Stegemann, *Die Entstehung der Qumrangemeinde* (Bonn: Rheinische Friedrich-Wilhelms-Universität, 1971).

2. See Schiffman, *Reclaiming the Dead Sea Scrolls*, 70–3, 80.

3. See ibid., 317–27.

4. See ibid., 397–9.

5. Translations of the Dead Sea Scrolls are from Florentino García Martínez, trans., *The Dead Sea Scrolls Translated*, translated into English by Wilfred G. E. Watson (Leiden: E. J. Brill, 1994).

6. See also 1QS III 11–2; IV 22; V 1–5, 8–12, 18–22; VI 14–5, 18–20; VIII 8–10, 16–9; X 10–1)

7. Frank M. Cross Jr., "Dead Sea Scrolls: Overview," in *Encyclopedia of Mormonism*, ed. Daniel H. Ludlow (New York: Macmillan, 1991), 1:362.

8. On the use of *Christ* in place of *Messiah* in the Book of Mormon, see Stephen D. Ricks, "Book of Mormon Prophets Knew before the Lord's Birth That His Name Would Be Jesus Christ. Did Old Testament Prophets Also Know?" *Ensign* (September 1984): 24-5.

9. See the outstanding study of the temple in the Book of Mormon by John W. Welch, "The Temple in the Book of Mormon," in *Temples of the Ancient World*, ed. Donald W. Parry (Salt Lake City: Deseret Book and FARMS, 1994), 297–387.

10. See David E. Aune, *Prophecy in Early Christianity and the Ancient Mediterranean World* (Grand Rapids, Mich.: Eerdmans, 1983), 342.

11. Josephus, *Jewish War*, trans. H. Thackeray and R. Marcus, Loeb Classical Library (1927), 2.159.

12. *1QpHabakkuk* II 2–3.

# CHAPTER 7

# PUTTING THE PIECES TOGETHER: DNA AND THE DEAD SEA SCROLLS

*Scott R. Woodward*

A number of questions concerning the origin and pro-duction of the Dead Sea Scrolls may be addressed using DNA analysis. These documents were for the most part written on what is thought to be goat- or sheepskin parch-ment. Based on radiocarbon and other analyses, these manuscripts date between the mid–second century B.C.E. and the first century C.E.[1] Under most conditions it would be remarkable that organic material, like parchment, would survive intact after such a long period of time. However, some of the material is remarkably well preserved because of the unique climate and storage conditions at Qumran. Because these parchments were produced from animal skins, they may contain remnant DNA molecules. Within the last decade, new techniques in molecular biology have

*Scott R. Woodward is associate professor of microbiology at Brigham Young University. This chapter is a revised version of "Analysis of Parchment Fragments from the Judean Desert Using DNA Techniques,"* in Current Research and Technological Developments on the Dead Sea Scrolls, *ed. Donald W. Parry and Stephen D. Ricks (Leiden: E. J. Brill, 1996), 215–38.*

been developed that have made it possible to recover DNA from ancient sources. The molecular analysis of ancient DNA (aDNA) from the Judean desert parchment fragments would enable us to establish a genetic signature unique for each manuscript. The precision of the DNA analysis will allow us to identify the species, population, and individual animal from which the parchment was produced.

## Background

The ability to recover biomolecules, most importantly DNA, from ancient remains has opened new research that has many implications.[2] Access to aDNA provides the opportunity to study the genetic material of past organisms and identify individual and population histories. Unfortunately, the DNA recovered from archaeological specimens is of such a degraded nature that the usual techniques associated with DNA fingerprinting cannot be used. However, modifications of the traditional procedures that involve using something called polymerase chain reaction (PCR) and short segments of unique DNA from the mitochondria and flanking short simple repeats from nuclear DNA can be used to identify the origin and identity of biological materials such as preserved skins or parchments.[3]

In 1984 the first reports on the retrieval of informative DNA sequences from an extinct animal appeared,[4] followed by the cloning of DNA from the skin of an ancient Egyptian mummy dated 2400 B.P. (before present).[5] The rapid degradation of biomolecules begins immediately following death. Except in unusual circumstances, this process continues unabated until the molecules return to a native state. DNA, found in large quantities in living tissue, degrades rapidly after death, and in most instances only small amounts of short DNA molecules can be recovered from dead tissue. This normally prevents recovery and analysis of DNA sequences from ancient tissue. However, the advent of PCR[6] in 1985 further opened the possibility of isolating DNA sequences in extracts in which the majority of the molecules are damaged and degraded. Theoretically, a single intact copy of a target DNA sequence, which only needs to be on the order of one hundred to two hundred base pairs in length, is sufficient for PCR, making it an ideal tool for aDNA studies. PCR products can be sequenced directly from a sample (this is preferable), or after cloning, making DNA sequence comparisons an extremely useful tool for the study of kinship relationships between individuals and populations. The amplification of mitochrondrial DNA (mtDNA) from ancient bones and teeth dated from 750 to 5450 years B.P. has been accomplished recently by a number of investigators.[7] aDNA has also been used in sex identification of skeletal remains.[8] PCR has been successfully applied to the analysis of ancient mtDNA from a variety of soft tissue remains, including a seven-thousand-year-old human brain,[9] an extinct marsupial wolf,[10] and—particularly relevant to this study—the preserved museum skins of over thirty kangaroo rats.[11] Numerous reports document the successful extraction and amplification of aDNA from museum skins and field-collected specimens,[12] including both naturally preserved (mummified) and actively treated skins from a wide variety of organisms, especially birds and mammals.[13] Some of these skins have been subjected to the same conditions that we expect to exist in the scroll parchments, and the extraction procedures for such specimens are not substantially different from those we have used in previous studies of aDNA.

## Methodology

Although there are many successful studies employing aDNA analysis, numerous difficulties and methodological problems still arise. The PCR technology is extremely sensitive and can be easily affected by contamination from nonrelevant DNA material. The source of contamination may be other personnel working in the field and laboratory or microorganisms such as bacteria. Another problem is the presence of inhibitors of unknown origin in aDNA extracts that interfere with the PCR reaction.[14] In our laboratories, all work is routinely carried out using rooms, equipment, and reagents kept only for aDNA analysis. All personnel wear masks and sterile gloves to minimize contamination, and extensive controls are routinely used in all stages of DNA extraction and amplification. Specimens are thoroughly cleaned before sampling, and only sterile instruments that have been exposed to ultraviolet light to destroy DNA are used. Approaches have been developed to overcome the inhibitor effect, either through dilution of the inhibitor prior to PCR[15] or alternate purification techniques. Contamination by contemporary human DNA will not pose a serious problem to this study because it is easy to differentiate the contaminating human DNA from the animal DNA obtained from the parchments.

The aDNA obtained from the parchment fragments may help answer some interesting questions like the following:

## What species of animals were used for parchment production?

Currently it is thought that most of the scrolls were written on goat- or sheepskins, but variations in texture, color, thickness, and follicle number and distribution in the surviving parchments may indicate that other skins were also used. On the basis of microscopic examination of the distribution of hair follicles remaining in the parchment fragments, Ryder[16] was able to determine four different groups that could have been the possible species of origin for twenty samples of parchment from the Dead Sea area. He determined that one sample group derived from calf, one from a fine-wooled sheep, one from a medium-wooled sheep, and one from a hairy animal that could have been either a sheep or a goat. However, the exact species identification is impossible using only microscopic examination.

It is likely that scrolls destined to contain religious writings were produced from ritually clean animals. According to Maimonides, "A scroll of the Law or phylacteries written on skins not expressly tanned for those purposed, is unfit for use."[17] Evidence from biblical sources and from at least one of the Judean desert scrolls (*Temple Scroll*) shows that very strict requirements were placed on the purity of animal skins. In particular, the skins brought into the temple or the temple city had extra requirements placed on their origin and preparation. According to Yadin, these skins had to be not only pure but "entirely holy and pure."[18] In the *Temple Scroll* this requirement is stressed:

> Skin, even if it was made from the hide of a clean animal, unless the animal had been sacrificed in the Temple [should not be brought to the Temple city]. Such ordinary skins are, indeed, clean for the need of all labour in other cities, but "into the city of my temple they shall not bring [them]."[19]

Some of the parchments used at Qumran may have had less strict requirements for cleanliness and purity applied to them. It was therefore possible to use skins from species of animals that were clean, but not necessarily ritually pure and used for sacrifice in the temple. These clean, but not temple-city-worthy animals could have included a number of animal species such as gazelle, ibex, dishon, or deer. By identifying the species of animal used for the production of a specific parchment, it may be possible to postulate a hierarchy of importance for the different manuscripts. Some would have been intended for use in the temple or synagogue and other important sites within the temple city or community, and others may have had lesser religious significance.

The Rockefeller Museum in Jerusalem, where thousands of scroll fragments are preserved. (Photograph courtesy Dana M. Pike.)

**How many different manuscripts are represented in the collection of fragments at the Rockefeller and Israel museums?**

Unfortunately, most of the recovered parchment material is quite fragmented, making it difficult to establish physically contiguous pieces of manuscripts. It is estimated that the approximately ten thousand fragments can be grouped into perhaps eight hundred different manuscripts, and it would be of tremendous value to be able to determine exactly which fragments belong together. Obtaining DNA signatures unique to each manuscript will make it possible to sort out the physical relationships of scroll fragments. Such information should prove particularly useful in sorting out the huge number of small fragments that cannot be confidently grouped on the basis of fragment shape, style of handwriting, or text, and it could provide unique insights into the subsequent interpretation of the scrolls.

**Which fragments can be grouped together as originating from the same manuscript because they are from identical or closely related parchments?**

Because individual animals can be identified by their unique genetic signature, it is theoretically possible to identify the unique origin of each of the parchment fragments based on their genetic information. Using the techniques of aDNA analysis, fragments belonging to the same or closely related skins can be grouped together. This could assist both in the reconstruction of manuscripts and in the verification of assemblies already made.

**Did more than one scribe work on a single document, or did different scribes use parchment originating from the same source for different manuscripts?**

There are examples in which two or more scribes worked on the same manuscript, as was the case with the *Temple Scroll*, *Thanksgiving Scroll*, and several other scrolls. If more than one scribe participated in the production of a single scroll, which was then subsequently damaged and is today quite fragmented, the critical analysis based only on paleography could falsely identify separate origins of the text.

Because of their size, some of the scrolls (i.e. the *Isaiah Scroll*, the *Manual of Discipline,* and the *Temple Scroll*) are composed of parchments produced from a number of different animals. The *Temple Scroll* is written on nineteen separate sheets of parchment, each one thirty-seven to sixty-one centimeters in length.[20] It is probable that no more than two or four sheets were derived from the same animal. Analysis of fragments from each section of these scrolls will allow us to determine the degree of relatedness of the parchments in a single scroll and whether they are derived from identical or closely related animals. This analysis could also be applied to repair patches that would give us information about where a scroll was when it was patched. Is the parchment for the patch from the same herd as the original manuscript? Does the patch represent a herd from a different region, reflecting mobility of either the original scroll or the herd? Perhaps parchment was a trade item that was brought from one or a number of different sources. The resulting data, revealing the level of relatedness of the parchment from a single scroll, will establish benchmarks valuable for the subsequent interpretation of the genetic data obtained by analysis of the aDNA from the fragments.

**Does the collection represent a library from a single locality, or is it a collection representing contributions from a wide region?**

Comparing DNA fingerprints recovered from the parchments and those obtained from archaeological remains of animals found in ancient sites throughout Israel can determine the origins of the parchment. In the ancient populations of domestic animals in Israel certain alleles (forms of a gene) likely became fixed by inbreeding in local herds. This is especially true if a group such as that at Qumran was isolated and closed.[21] Biblical examples of the importance of separating flocks and herds are reflected in Genesis 13:5–9, when Abram and Lot separate their herds to different locales, and again in Genesis 30:40, when Jacob separates his herds from those belonging to Laban.

It was apparently critical that animals for the production of skins to be used in Jerusalem, the temple city, were derived from flocks and animals that were "known to their ancestors."[22] This suggests that flocks and herds were carefully observed and may have been guarded against "contaminating" crossbreeding. Such patterns of husbandry would effectively produce closed breeding groups with predictable genetic consequences. Fixed allele patterns would establish specific markers in the population that could be used to identify and differentiate local herds. Analysis of aDNA extracted from goat bones excavated at Qumran and other archaeological sites within present-day Israel could reveal any fixed allele patterns and will be compared to the alleles found in the parchments. An aDNA analysis will determine if the sampled parchments were produced locally at Qumran or collected from different locations. A test of the sensitivity of this procedure could be performed comparing genetic fingerprints from scrolls that were likely composed at Qumran, such as the *Rule of the Community* (1QS), and others that were possibly brought to Qumran from another location in Palestine, such as the *Isaiah Scroll* (1QIsaᵃ).[23] Another potential source of information about the origin of manuscripts is a comparison of DNA sequence with "autograph" documents, several of which may now have been identified in the Qumran collections.[24] These autographs may be considered to have been authored by the people at Qumran and would provide a genetic fingerprint of the parchment used by these individuals.

The molecular identification of parchment fragments involved a number of complex steps. We first demonstrated the ability to isolate and amplify aDNA from parchment on "modern parchment," animal skins that have been treated in a similar way to that which we believe was practiced anciently. To extract the DNA, the skin fragments were pulverized in liquid nitrogen, dissolved and lysed in a highly chaotropic solution and the DNA recovered by collection on silica beads. We have extracted DNA from museum skins of rabbits and commercially prepared deer and sheep skins. These fragments were sequenced and shown to be specific for rabbit, deer, and sheep, respectively, and these procedures were then used to obtain aDNA from the ancient parchment.

After we demonstrated that it was actually possible to obtain DNA from treated skins, the next step was to identify in modern goats—both domestic and wild—and other potential parchment sources the appropriate DNA sequence changes, or polymorphisms, capable of differentiating individual, herd, or species. DNA was isolated from modern domestic goats, wild goats, sheep, ibex, and other animals possibly used for parchment production and then amplified using the polymerase chain reaction (PCR). From our preliminary results it is clear that unique DNA regions will be identified that will give good differentiation at the species and herd level.

### Results

We have begun to extract aDNA from small portions of parchment fragments of the Dead Sea Scrolls, amplify biologically active DNA using the polymerase chain reaction (PCR), obtain DNA sequences, and identify unique genetic signatures of the fragments. This has shown that the process is feasible and can be used to reestablish the physical relationships of scroll fragments that may help clarify the translation and interpretation of the scrolls.

We have extracted DNA from eleven small pieces (approximately 0.5 cm$^2$) of parchment from the area and time period corresponding to the Dead Sea Scroll parchments. DNA from these fragments has been successfully amplified and sequenced. The sequence of six of these fragments is most closely related to, but not identical with, that of both wild and domestic goats. It is significantly different from the human sequence, demonstrating that the parchment material was not contaminated by human DNA either in the handling of the parchment during collection or during the laboratory manipulations. The number of differences between the aDNA and the contemporary goat DNA is greater than is generally expected because of the accumulated normal evolutionary mutations over the two-thousand-year interval. The aDNA is probably not from the same species as the contemporary goat samples. However, fewer differences occur between the ancient sample and the modern goat than between the ancient sample and either sheep or cow. This suggests a closer relationship to a goatlike animal than to a cow or sheep. We then compared the first two of the eleven fragments with sequences that we have determined for the modern ibex and gazelle. These comparisons indicate the possibility that these fragments derived from either a gazelle or ibexlike animal.

We have also examined six fragments from five different sheets of the *Temple Scroll*. These have all been shown to be derived from goat. For these fragments, no difference exists between ancient and modern goats at this gene locus. We are currently in the process of identifying individual DNA polymorphisms in those fragments to determine the degree of relatedness of the animals used to produce the parchment in the scroll.

We have also been able to isolate and amplify DNA from archaeological bones of ibex and goats found at Masada. In most of the instances, horn cores that have been identified by species have been used as the source of DNA. This demonstrates our ability to recover from ancient animal remains the necessary genetic information that will enable us to compare the scroll fragments with the animals from which they were derived. This will allow geographical localization of the parchment sources.

In conclusion, we have demonstrated the ability to recover aDNA from the parchment on which the Dead Sea Scrolls were written. We have also shown that it is possible to recover authentic sequence from this material and use it to make comparisons with other sequences. Our early results indicate that the skins from which the first two ancient fragments were derived are not domestic or wild goat, but are likely a wild species of gazelle or ibex. We have also determined that seven other random fragments are derived from goat; six of these fragments come from the *Temple Scroll*. These analyses differ from the classifications made using microscopic analyses of similar parchment fragments from the same area by Ryder.[25] We have not yet identified any parchment from a species of sheep.

This project is the beginning of a fruitful collaboration that will continue over the next few years. We hope that the analysis of DNA from parchment fragments will add a new level of critical analysis to scroll scholarship.

## Notes

Funding for this research was made available through the Foundation for Ancient Research and Mormon Studies and the Dead Sea Scrolls Foundation.

1. See G. Bonani et al., "Radiocarbon Dating of the Dead Sea Scrolls," *Atiqot* 20 (1991): 27–32; G. A. Rodley, "An Assessment of the Radiocarbon Dating of the Dead Sea Scrolls," *Radiocarbon* 35 (1993): 335–8.

2. See Bernd Herrmann and Susanne Hummel, introduction to *Ancient DNA*, ed. Bernd Herrmann and Susanne Hummel (New York: Springer-Verlag, 1994), 1–12.

3. See Francis X. Villablanca, "Spatial and Temporal Aspects of Populations Revealed by Mitochondrial DNA," in *Ancient DNA*, ed. Herrmann and Hummel, 31–58.

4. See Russell Higuchi et al., "DNA Sequences from Quagga, an Extinct Member of the Horse Family," *Nature* 312 (1984): 282–4.

5. See Svante Pääbo, "Molecular Cloning of Ancient Egyptian Mummy DNA," *Nature* 314 (1985): 644–5; Jörg T. Epplen, "Simple Repeat Loci as Tools for Genetic Identification," in *Ancient DNA*, ed. Herrmann and Hummel, 13–30.

6. See Randall K. Saiki et al., "Enzymatic Amplification of Beta-Globin Genomic Sequences and Restriction Site Analysis for Diagnosis of Sickle Cell Anemia," *Science* 230 (1985): 1350–4.

7. See Erika Hagelberg, B. Sykes, and R. Hedges, "Ancient Bone DNA Amplified," *Nature* 342 (1989): 485; Erika Hagelberg et al., "Ancient Bone DNA: Techniques and Applications," *Philosophical Transactions of the Royal Society of London B* 333 (1991): 339–407; Erika Hagelberg and J. B. Clegg, "Isolation and Characterization of DNA from Archaeological Bone," *Proceedings of the Royal Society of London B* 244 (1991): 45–50; S. Horai et al., "DNA Amplification from Ancient Human Skeletal Remains and Their Sequence Analysis," *Proceedings of the Japanese Academy of Science* 65 (1989): 229–33; G. Hanni et al., "Amplification of Mitochondrial DNA Fragments from Ancient Human Teeth and Bone," *C. R. Academy of Science*, 3rd ser., 310 (1990): 356–70; Susanne Hummel and Bernd Herrmann, "Y-Chromosome-Specific DNA Amplified in Ancient Human Bone," *Naturwissenschaften* 78 (1991): 266–7; D. A. Lawlor et al., "Ancient HLA Genes from 7500-year-old Archaeological Remains," *Nature* 349 (1991): 785–8; E. Beraud-Columb, J. M. Tiercy, and G. Querat, "Human Beta-thalassemia

Gene Detected in 7000-year-old Fossil Bones," in *Proceedings of the 3rd International Congress on Human Paleontology, Jerusalem, Israel, August 23–28, 1992* (1992), 146 (abstract); K. Thomas et al., "Spatial and Temporal Continuity of Kangaroo Rat Populations Shown by Sequencing," *Journal of Molecular Evolution* 31 (1990): 101–12; Scott R. Woodward et al., "Amplification of Nuclear DNA from Teeth and Soft Tissue," *PCR Methods and Applications* 3/4 (1994): 244–7; and Svante Pääbo, Russell G. Higuchi, and Allan C. Wilson, "Ancient DNA and the Polymerase Chain Reaction," *Journal of Biological Chemistry* 264 (1989): 9709–12.

8. See Hummel and Herrmann, "Y-chromosome-specific," 266–7; Svante Pääbo, "Ancient DNA: Extraction, Characterization, Molecular Cloning and Enzymatic Amplification," *Proceedings of the National Academy of Sciences* 83 (1989): 1939–43.

9. See Lawlor et al., "Ancient HLA Genes," 785–8.

10. See R. H. Thomas et al., "DNA Phylogeny of the Extinct Marsupial Wolf," *Nature* 340 (1989): 465–7.

11. See K. Thomas et al., "Spatial and Temporal Continuity," 101–12.

12. See R. H. Thomas et al., "DNA Phylogeny"; K. Thomas et al., "Spatial and Temporal Continuity"; M. Culver, personal communication.

13. See K. Thomas et al., "Spatial and Temporal Continuity."

14. See Hagelberg and Clegg, "Isolation and Characterization," 45–50; Pääbo, "Ancient DNA: Extraction."

15. See Hagelberg and Clegg, "Isolation and Characterization"; Pääbo, "Ancient DNA: Extraction."

16. See W. Ryder, "Remains Derived from Skin," in *Microscopic Studies of Ancient Skins* (Oxford: Oxford University Press, 1965).

17. Maimonides, as quoted by Yigael Yadin in *The Temple Scroll* (Jerusalem: Israel Exploration Society, 1983), 1:315.

18. Yadin, *Temple Scroll*, 1:309.

19. Ibid.

20. See ibid., 1:9–10.

21. See James H. Charlesworth, *Jesus and the Dead Sea Scrolls* (New York: Doubleday, 1992), xxxiii; Emmanuel Tov, "Textual

Witness of the Bible," in *Textual Criticism of the Hebrew Bible.* (Minneapolis: Fortress Press, 1992), 102.

22. Josephus, *Antiquities of the Jews,* trans. R. Marcus, Loeb Classical Library (1966), 12.146.

23. Norman Golb, "The Problem of Origin and Identification of the Dead Sea Scrolls," *Proceedings of the American Philosophical Society* 124 (1980): 1–24; Norman Golb, "Who Hid the Dead Sea Scrolls?" *Biblical Archaeology* 48 (June 1985): 68–82.

24. See Golb, "The Problem of Origin," and Golb, "Who Hid the Dead Sea Scrolls?"

25. See Ryder, "Remains Derived from Skin."

# CHAPTER 8

# THE FARMS-BYU DEAD SEA SCROLLS ELECTRONIC DATABASE

*Donald W. Parry*
*Steven W. Booras*
*E. Jan Wilson*

Scholars and interested nonscholars can now access the Dead Sea Scrolls on computer. The Foundation for Ancient Research and Mormon Studies (FARMS), in conjunction with Brigham Young University and other parties,[1] has developed a computerized reference library of Dead Sea Scrolls materials that includes photographs of the scrolls and scroll fragments, transcriptions of the writings on the scrolls into modern Hebrew characters and English translations of the Hebrew.[2] For the first time, students, scholars, and informed laypersons will be able to access the Dead Sea Scrolls quickly and effectively via the computer with the FARMS-BYU Dead Sea Scrolls Electronic Database. The combination of modern computer power and sophisticated text-manipulating software offers the prospect of combining

*Donald W. Parry is assistant professor of Hebrew language and literature at Brigham Young University, Steven W. Booras is electronic projects specialist at the Foundation for Ancient Research and Mormon Studies, and E. Jan Wilson is associate director of the FARMS Center for the Electronic Preservation of Ancient Religious Texts.*

all these materials into a database that can be analyzed simultaneously and instantaneously by scholars and researchers at a relatively low cost.

In the past, limited access to the scrolls hindered the studies of scholars and students of the Dead Sea Scrolls. In recent years the situation has improved somewhat because of increasing publication of DSS material. The database now makes it possible for individuals to study the scrolls on computer. The database will not offer interpretations or scholarly analyses of the scrolls. It aims only to provide comprehensive reference materials in the most accessible format possible. It does not pretend to offer authoritative or new readings of texts. It simply provides the most accurate possible readings that have already been offered by DSS scholars.

## Computer Power

The database uses the WordCruncher™ search engine, a program developed at BYU, and provides the ability to

- access large quantities of material, including both text and photographs;
- search the text for words and phrases;
- display the photographs of the scrolls and fragments;
- store and retrieve earlier searches;
- copy blocks of material to be stored on the user's disk or hard drive and print the materials on the user's printer;
- find the number of times a given word is attested in a single document or in a number of documents and study its usage in various contextual settings to determine meaning;
- research and compare items in a way not possible a generation ago.

## The Computerized Photographs

The database contains over eleven hundred photographs of the scrolls that were scanned from negatives and transparencies belonging to the Ancient Biblical Manuscript Center collection in Claremont, California. Dr. James Sanders, president of the Ancient Biblical Manuscript Center, and his staff have graciously allowed the use of these photographs in the database.[3] The selection of images includes photographs from the Palestine Archaeological Museum (held at the Rockefeller Museum), the Israel Antiquities Authority, and the Shrine of the Book. The database allows the user to view and manipulate the photograph on the computer. For instance, the user is able to magnify the photograph and study it very closely.

Fig. 1. Computerized image of a portion of 1QSa

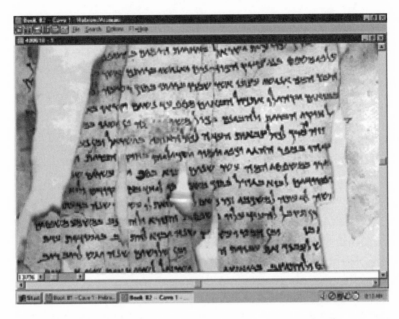

Fig. 2. Magnified image of a portion of 1QSa

**Searching the Text**

Both the Hebrew text (transcription) of the scrolls and the English translation may be searched for words and phrases. A simple word search or a search for a sophisticated phrase search may be conducted throughout the entire database. The results of the search ("hits") are shown immediately and can be viewed on the computer screen. The results may be printed or stored on the disk for recall at a later time.

# Conclusion

The database includes numerous other features that will assist serious students in their study of the Dead Sea Scrolls, such as the ability to add the user's research notes to

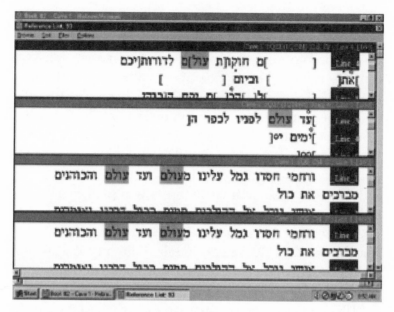

Fig. 3. Six occurrences of the word עולם

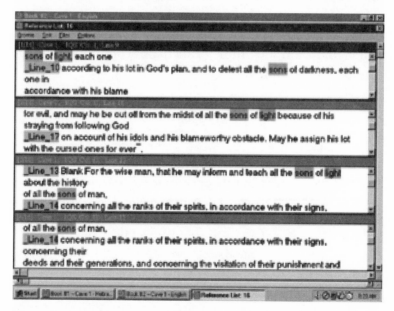

Fig. 4. Searching for the words *sons* and *light* within ten words of each other

the database or to conduct wild-card searches. External programs can be executed while using the database, and a Hebrew lexicon can be referenced. In addition, the "database supports the synchronization of two or more files simultaneously if they possess marked codes. . . . As the user scrolls down one text, the computer automatically repositions the other text(s) to the same section as the text being scrolled."[4]

The database brings scholarship and state-of-the-art technology closer together. When it is published in 1997 or early 1998, we expect that its users will gain many new insights as they study the scrolls. We may also see new discoveries and contributions in related fields of study, including the Old Testament, Judaism, linguistics, history, Near Eastern languages, early Christianity, and religious studies.

This same technology may eventually be used to study documents from other cultures and peoples, such as the ancient Maya of Mesoamerica or the early Chaldean Christians of Northern Persia. The Foundation for Ancient Research and Mormon Studies anticipates continuing its pioneering efforts in this direction.

## Notes

1. We acknowledge the work, dedication, and expertise of several individuals who have made the dream regarding the database become a reality. We appreciate the collaborative efforts and ongoing encouragement of both Emanuel Tov, editor in chief of the Dead Sea Scrolls publication project and professor at Hebrew University, Jerusalem, and Weston W. Fields, executive director of the DSS Foundation. We are grateful to Stephen J. Pfann of the Center for the Study of Early Christianity for the DSS transcription files and to James A. Sanders, president of the Ancient Biblical Manuscript Center in Claremont, California, for the scroll and fragment photographs. We also recognize FARMS and

BYU, both of which have contributed many resources in the form of personnel, services, and consultative assistance. In particular, we thank Noel B. Reynolds, professor of political science at BYU, president of FARMS, and producer of the FARMS-BYU Dead Sea Scrolls Electronic Database; Monte F. Shelley, director of Instructional Applications Services at BYU; and his colleagues James S. Rosenvall, manager of WordCruncher™ development team, William A. Barrett, associate chair of the computer science department, and Daniel R. Bartholomew and Jason W. Dzubak, senior programmers. We also wish to thank Dana Pike, assistant professor of ancient scripture at BYU; Terry Szink, Ph.D. candidate in Near Eastern languages and cultures at UCLA; and Kerry M. Muhlestein, a BYU graduate student in Near Eastern studies, for their professional assistance.

2. The database currently features only nonbiblical texts from the eleven caves of Qumran.

3. See Stephen A. Reed, *The Dead Sea Scrolls Catalogue: Documents, Photographs and Museum Inventory Numbers* (Atlanta: Scholars Press, 1994).

4. Donald W. Parry and Steven W. Booras, "The Dead Sea Scrolls CD-ROM Database Project," in *Current Research and Technological Developments on the Dead Sea Scrolls*, ed. Donald W. Parry and Stephen D. Ricks (New York: E. J. Brill, 1996), 250.

# Index

anointing 156, 161, 164, 184
Antiochus IV 18
apocryphal texts
11, 12, 53, 67
apograph texts 54
apostasy 98
aqueduct system 8
Arab-Israeli conflict 4
Aramaic 11, 52
*Aramaic Apocalypse* 141–6
on Messianic expectations
183
autograph texts 54, 199

**B**

Babylonia
origin of Essenes 15
Balaam's oracle 117, 120
baptism 95
Bar Kokhba. *See* ben Kosiba,
Simeon
Bar Kokhba Revolt 10–1
*Barki Nafshi*
xii, xviii, 110, 111
bath. *See* ritual bath
Belial 92 n. 13
ben Kosiba, Simeon 11
*Berakhot Milḥamah* 128
Bethel 13
bishop, Christian 33
Book of Mormon
compared with Dead Sea
Scrolls 179–83
Book of the Parables of Enoch
118
Broshi, Magen 9

**C**

Cairo Codex of the Prophets
47
calendar 35–7, 102, 107
tenth jubilee 159. *See also*
festivals
Canaan, curse on 120
canon, open 38
Cave 1 xiii, 4, 7, 49, 127
excavation of 7–10
Cave 3 12, 49, 179
Cave 4 11, 49, 99
Cave 11 12, 29, 49, 101, 103
CD. *See Damascus Document*
celibacy 35. *See also* marriage
cemeteries 34
Chaldeans 109
cisterns 119
cloning 193
coenaculum. *See* triclinium
Collection of Blessings. *See*
*Rule of the Blessings*
commentaries 53, 120. *See
also Genesis Commentary;
Habakkuk Commentary;
Isaiah Commentary; Psalms
Commentary*
communal meal 9, 26–
7, 38, 106
computerized reference
library 207–16
*Copper Scroll* 12
covenant Israel
1, 30, 32, 34, 96–
7, 106, 111, 128, 179–80
Covenant, Renewed 34
creator 76
Cross, Frank Moore 13

Prince of the Congregation
126–8, 132, 153–8
as Davidic Messiah 155
private property 106
property, common ownership
22–3
prophecy, gift of 186
prophet 156, 160–6
belief in advent of 31, 147–
8
discernment by High Priest
153
Psalms 98
psalms, Davidic 101–2
*Psalms Commentary* 53
*Psalms Scroll* 48, 103
on Davidic psalms 101
Pseudepigraphic texts
11, 53, 67
punishment at Qumran 104

## Q

Qumran ix, 2–3, 8–10
aerial view of ruins 187
history of community 15–
20, 38
map 119
populated by Essenes 13–
24, 74

## R

radiocarbon analysis 191
Renewed Covenant 34
repair patches 198
repentance 96, 107–8
resurrection 25, 86–9, 133.
ritual bath 8, 26, 107, 119

ritual meal 14. *See also*
communal meal; Messi-
anic banquet
ritually clean animals
195, 199
Rockefeller Museum
19, 63, 196, 209
Romans 39, 109
*Rule of the Blessings* 126
*Rule of the Community* 4
composed at Qumran 199
discovered in Cave 1 4
oldest copy 148, 165
on afterlife 88
on covenant Israel 180
on fate of wicked 89
on God's grace 81
on God's omniscience 76
on initiation 106
on law of Moses 103, 181
on multiple Messiahs 147
on obedience to God's will
83
on prayer 100, 105
on predestination 24, 79
on property 23
on ritual cleaning 26, 108
on spitting 30
on temple worship 184
on the "Prophet like Moses"
160, 163
on war between good and
evil 185
*Rule of the Congregation*
182, 209, 210
on communal meal 38
on "Messiah of Israel" 125
on Messianic banquet 150
on nature of Messiah 150

made of goatskin parch-
ment 201
on end-time temple 39
on ritually clean skins 195
on toilet procedures 29
worked on by more than
one scribe 197
temple worship 32, 184
Ten Commandments 55, 105
*Testament of Levi* 136–7
on "Priestly Messiah" 136–
8
*Testaments of the XII Patriarchs*
on "Priestly Messiah" 137
Tetragrammaton xvii, 62, 71.
*See also* divine name
textual variants 148. *See also*
scribal errors, variant
readings
*Thanksgiving Hymns*
4, 110, 111
columns renumbered 91
on afterlife 88
on divine assistance 85
on God's grace 80
on God's power 76
on obedience 84
on predestination 78
on premortal life 77
on resurrection 86
worked on by more than
one scribe 197
theological changes 55, 61
*Three Tongues of Fire* 152
Timotheus I
describes discovery of
manuscripts 3
toilet habits
Sabbath 28–30
Torah 108

Tov, Emanuel xi–xii
transcriptions of Dead Sea
Scrolls 207
translations of Dead Sea
Scrolls xviii, 207
triclinium 9, 42 n. 12

## U

United Nations 4
Urim 154

## V

variant readings 54–7
causes 57
in Samaritan Pentateuch 55
New Testament 55–6
theological changes 55, 61.
*See also* textual variants

## W

wadi 2
Wadi Murabbaʾat 10, 50, 66
war, final 131
war between good and evil
185–6
war in heaven 80
*War Scroll* 142, 152, 184
discovered in Cave 1 4
lost ending 128
on anointing 161
on destruction of wicked 88
on final battle 39
on God's power 76
on predestination 93 n. 17
on priestly anointing 184
on temple worship 32

# The Foundation for Ancient Research and Mormon Studies (FARMS)

The Foundation for Ancient Research and Mormon Studies encourages and supports research and publication about the Book of Mormon, Another Testament of Jesus Christ, and other ancient scriptures.

FARMS is a nonprofit, tax-exempt educational foundation, established in 1979. Its main research interests in the scriptures include ancient history, language, literature, culture, geography, politics, religion, and law. Although research on such subjects is of secondary importance when compared with the spiritual and eternal messages of the scriptures, solid scholarly research can supply certain kinds of useful information, even if only tentatively, concerning many significant and interesting questions about the ancient backgrounds, origins, composition, and meanings of scripture.

The work of the Foundation rests on the premise that the Book of Mormon and other scriptures were written by prophets of God. Belief in this premise—in the divinity of scripture—is a matter of faith. Religious truths require divine witness to establish the faith of the believer. While scholarly research cannot replace that witness, such studies may reinforce and encourage individual testimonies by fostering understanding and appreciation of the scriptures. It is hoped that this information will help people to "come unto Christ" (Jacob 1:7) and to understand and take more seriously these ancient witnesses of the atonement of Jesus Christ, the Son of God.

The Foundation works to make interim and final reports about its research available widely, promptly, and economically, both in scholarly and popular formats. FARMS publishes information about the Book of Mormon and other ancient scripture in the *Insights* newsletter; books and research papers; *FARMS Review of Books; Journal of Book of Mormon Studies;* reprints of published scholarly papers; and videos and audiotapes. FARMS also supports the preparation of the *Collected Works of Hugh Nibley.*

To facilitate the sharing of information, FARMS sponsors lectures, seminars, symposia, firesides, and radio and television broadcasts in which research findings are communicated to working scholars and to anyone interested in faithful, reliable information about the scriptures. Through Research Press, a publishing arm of the Foundation, FARMS publishes materials addressed primarily to working scholars.

The Foundation is independent of all other organizations and does not speak for any other organization. FARMS is supported solely by subscriptions, sales, and private donations.

For more information about the Foundation and its activities, contact the FARMS office at 1-800-327-6715 or (801) 373-5111.